GW00391350

Contents

Themed Poetry 131

3. Read All About It! 157

4. Dabble in Drama! 181

Don't Forget 212

5. Tell Me a Story 213

x

The authors and publisher wish to thank the following for permission to reproduce copyright material:

Extract from *Fast Food Nation* by Eric Schlosser (Penguin Books Ltd, 2001). Copyright © Eric Schlosser, 2001. Reproduced by permission of Penguin Books Ltd. Extract from *Chinese Cinderella* by Adeline Yen Mah (Penguin, 1999). Copyright © Adeline Yen Mah 1999. Reproduced by permission of Penguin Books Ltd. Extract from *What I Was* by Meg Rosoff (Puffin, 2007). Copyright © Meg Rosoff, 2007. Reproduced by permission of Penguin Books Ltd. Extract from *The Great Stink* by Clare Clark (Viking Books 2006). Copyright © Clare Clark, 2005. Reproduced by permission of Penguin Books Ltd and Aitken Alexander. Extract from *Fever Pitch* by Nick Hornby (first published by Victor Gollancz 1992, Penguin Books 2000). Copyright © Nick Hornby, 1992. 'A Talk in the Dark', by Walter Macken from *The Grass of the People* (Brandon 1998) reproduced by permission of Brandon Books. Extract from *The Princess Bride, S. Morgenstern's Classic Tale of True Love and High Adventure*, abridged by William Goldman. Published by Bloomsbury Publishing. Extract from *Safe* by Kate Hanney. Reproduced by permission of the author. 'Christopher' by Eoin Colfer © 2008. Reprinted by permission of Eoin Colfer. Extract from *William's Version* by Jan Mark. Reprinted by kind permission of Pearson. Extract from *The Joshua Files: Invisible City* Copyright © M.G. Harris, 2008. Reproduced with the permission of Scholastic Ltd. All rights reserved. Extract from *The Secret World of the Irish Male* by Joseph O'Connor, published by New Island Books. © Joseph O'Connor, 1994. Extract from *An Unsung Hero: Tom Crean, Antarctic Survivor* by Michael Smith. Published by The Collins Press. Extract from *Scorpia* by Anthony Horowitz. Text © Anthony Horowitz. Reproduced by permission of Walker Books Ltd, London SE11 5HJ. Excerpt from *A Tree Grows in Brooklyn* by Betty Smith. Copyright © Betty Smith 1943, 1947. Copyright renewed 1971 by Betty Smith (Finch). Reprinted by permission of HarperCollins Publishers Ltd.

Extract from *Confessions of Georgia Nicolson: Angus, Thongs and Full-Frontal Snogging* by Louise Rennison. Copyright © Louise Rennison, 2001. Reprinted by permission of HarperCollins Publishers Ltd. 'The Furnace Monster', from *Loser* by Jerry Spinelli. Copyright © Jerry Spinelli, 2003. Reprinted by permission of HarperCollins Publishers Ltd. Extract from *Private Peaceful* by Michael Morpurgo. Copyright © Michael Morpurgo, 2003. Reprinted by permission of HarperCollins Publishers Ltd. Extract from *Witch Child* by Celia Rees. Published by Bloomsbury Publishing. Extract from *Round Ireland with a Fridge* by Tony Hawks, published by Ebury Press. Reprinted by permission of The Random House Group Ltd. Extract from *Neither Here Nor There* by Bill Bryson, published by Black Swan. Reprinted by permission of The Random House Group Ltd. Extract from *I Want to Live* by Nina Lugovskaya, published by Doubleday. Reprinted by permission of The Random House Group Ltd. Extract from 'His First Flight' from *The Short Stories of Liam O'Flaherty* by Liam O'Flaherty, published by Jonathan Cape. Reprinted by permission of The Random House Group Ltd. 'Rocket Science' by Jeanne Willis reproduced by kind permission of Faber and Faber Ltd.

'A Plate of Peas' by Rick Beyer, published as part of *True Tales of American Life*, reproduced by kind permission of Faber and Faber Ltd. *The Butterfly* by Margit Koretzová and 'The Butterfly' by Pavel Friedman from *I Have Not Seen a Butterfly Around Here: Children's Drawings and Poems from Terezín* included by permission of the Jewish Museum in Prague. Front cover of *Private Peaceful* by Michael Morpurgo reproduced by permission of HarperCollins Publishers Ltd. Front cover of *The Amulet of Samarkand* by Jonathon Stroud published by Doubleday reproduced by permission of Random House. Front cover of *The Goose Girl* by Shannon Hale, *A Gathering Light* by Jennifer Donnelly, *Pirates* by Celia Rees and *Witch Child* by Celia Rees all reproduced by permission from Bloomsbury. Front cover of *The Fire-Eaters* by David Almond reproduced by permission of Hodder & Stoughton Ltd. The front cover of *Northern Lights* by Philip Pullman reproduced by permission of Scholastic Children's Books. The front cover of *The Joshua Files Invisible City* by M.G. Harris reproduced with the permission of Scholastic Ltd. Front cover of *The Boy in the Striped Pyjamas* by John Boyne reproduced by permission of Random House. Front cover of *Artemis Fowl* by Eoin Colfer reproduced by permission of Penguin Books Ltd. Front cover of *Inkheart* by Cornelia Funke, with cover illustration created by Carol Lawson, and front cover of *Martyn Pig*, by Kevin Brooks, reproduced by permission of Chicken House Publishing Ltd. Front cover of *Safe* by Kate Hanney, with cover image by Michael Hanney, reproduced by permission of the author. 'Never Blood so Red' by Grandfather Koori from *Inside Black Australia – An Anthology of Aboriginal Poetry* edited by Kevin Gilbert. Reproduced with permission by Penguin Group (Australia). 'Hugger Mugger' from Hot Dog and Other Stories by Kit Wright (Kestrel, 1981). Copyright © Kit Wright, 1981. Reproduced by permission of Penguin Books Ltd. 'The Mewlips' from *The Adventures of Tom Bombadil* by J.R.R. Tolkien © 1961 J.R.R. Tolkien. Reproduced by permission of HarperCollins Publishers Ltd. 'My Ship' from *Come Softly to My Wake* by Christy Brown, published by Secker & Warburg. Reprinted by permission of The Random House Group Ltd. 'Midsummer Tobago' by Derek Walcott, published as part of *Collected Poems 1948-1984* reproduced by kind permission of Faber and Faber Ltd. 'Night Mail' by W. H. Auden, published as part of *Collected Poems*, reproduced by kind permission of Faber and Faber Ltd. 'O What is That Sound' by W. H. Auden, published as part of *Collected Poems*, reproduced by kind permission of Faber and Faber Ltd. 'King of the Kurzel' from So Far So Good: Poems by Mick Gowar, reproduced with the permission of Mick Gowar. © Mick Gowar. 'What Is … the Sun?', by Wes Magee from *The Very Best of Wes Magee* reproduced with the permission of Wes Magee. 'The Listeners' by Walter de la Mare, from *The Complete Poems of Walter de la Mare*. Reprinted with permission of The Literary Trustees of Walter de la Mare and the Society of Authors as their representative. 'The Terrible People' by Ogden Nash, from *Candy Is Dandy: The Best of Ogden Nash* (1994). Published by André Deutsch. 'Hairstyle' by John Agard (Copyright © John Agard , 1996) reproduced by kind permission of John Agard c/o Caroline Sheldon Literary Agency Limited. 'Name Calling' by Charles Thomson reprinted with permission of the author. 'Awakening' reproduced with permission of Dorothy Jenkinson. 'Odours Savours Sweet' by A. S. Byatt from *Sightlines*, edited by P. D. James and Harriet Hervey Wood, used by permission of The Peters Fraser and Dunlop Group Ltd. 'The Ugly Child' by Elizabeth Jennings, from *The Secret Brother and Other Poems for Children* (Dufour Editions, 1966). 'Exile' by Moniza Alvi, from *Split World: Poems, 1990–2005* (Bloodaxe Books, 2008). 'The People of the Other Village' from *Split Horizon: Poems by Thomas Lux*. Copyright © 1994 by Thomas Lux. Reprinted by permission of Houghton Mifflin Harcourt Publishing. 'Four Seasons Haiku' by Adrian Henri, from *The Works: Every Kind of Poem You Will Ever Need for the Literacy Hour* ed. by Paul Cookson. 'Poem' by William Carlos Williams, from *Collected Poems* (2000). Reproduced with permission of Carcanet Press Limited. 'Back in the Playground Blues' from *On the Beach at Cambridge* (© Adrian Mitchell (1984) is reproduced by permission of PFD (www.pdf.co.uk) on behalf of the Estate of Adrian Mitchell Educational Health Warning! None of Adrian Mitchell's poems to be used in connection with any examinations whatsoever! 'Haiku', 'Acrostics' and 'Blood Is an Acquired Taste', by Roger McGough from *Collected Poems* (© Roger McGough (2004)) are reproduced by permission of PFD (www.pdf.co.uk) on behalf of Roger McGough. Extracts from *The Field* and *Sive* by John B. Keane, copyright © John B. Keane, 1990. Reprinted by kind permission of Mercier Press Ltd, Cork. Extract from *Billy Elliot* by Melvin Burgess, based on the screenplay by Lee Hall. Reprinted by permission of Chicken House. Extract from *Blood Brothers* by Willy Russell, published by Methuen Drama, an imprint of A & C Black Publishers. Extract from *Skungpoomery* by Ken Campbell, published by Methuen Drama, an imprint of A & C Black Publishers. Extract from *The Virtuous Burglar* by Dario Fo, from *Dario Fo Plays: I*, ed. Stuart Hood. Published by Methuen Drama, an imprint of A & C Black Publishers. Extract from *The Play of the Silver Sword* by Stuart Henson, Pearson Education Limited. Extract from *Father Ted*, written by Graham Linehan and Arthur Mathews, reprinted by permission of the authors and Hat Trick Productions. Indesit advert reproduced by permission of Indesit Company UK Limited. Adidas advertisement reproduced by permission of Adidas. Advertisements for Surf and Persil included with permission from Lever Fabergé. Advertisement for Danone included with permission from Danone Ireland. Advertisement for Rockport Shoes reprinted by permission of Reebok. Front cover of the Irish Independent reproduced by kind permission of the editor. Front cover of the Irish Times reproduced by kind permission of the editor. Front cover of the Irish Examiner reproduced by kind permission of the editor. Front cover of the Irish Mirror reproduced by kind permission of the editor. Irish Times article 'U2 to give €5m for music tuition', by Genevieve Carbery. Reproduced by permission of the author. Irish Daily Star article 'We'll Give Our Bands €5m', with accompanying image. Reproduced by permission of the editor.

Getty, Corbis, Alamy, iStockphoto, The Scott Polar Research Institute, Bridgeman, Picture Desk, Photocall, The President's Office, Moviestore Collection, The Kobal Collection.

Introduction

In this Second Edition of *Dive In*, you will find:

- A **wide variety of material** from classic extracts to contemporary blogs
- A range of material and activities **appropriate to any group**
- Stimulating extracts tailored to **average class times**
- **Inventive activities** which appeal to all interests
- Reading used as a **springboard** for Personal Writing
- A challenging and relevant **new selection of poetry** to engage readers
- Clear and concise explanations of **key poetic concepts,** creativity encouraged through **DIY Poetry Workshop**s
- Updated, innovative and interactive **Media and Advertising tasks**
- Dynamic and **entertaining Drama** material
- Enticing **new Fiction extracts** to inspire further reading
- **Integrated grammar** re-enforced by rewarding group exercises

Remember!

- Do not feel you must use *all* the material in this book!
- Every class should **select** material to suit their needs and preferences.

Most extracts are followed by four sets of activities:

 Short exploratory questions.

 Activities for *you* to do!

 Questions to make you think.

 Things for the class to talk about.

You will see the following symbol to indicate that there are additional materials in the Teacher's Resources booklet: **R**

Take a Dip!

In this chapter you will come across many types of **writing**, including:

- Diaries
- Biographies and autobiographies
- Memoirs
- Anecdotes

You will **learn** how to:

- Brainstorm
- Plan paragraphs
- Create characters
- Tell stories
- Come to grips with grammar

Confessions of Georgia Nicolson

Louise Rennison

A diary is a written record that some people keep of their daily lives. This record can be a very simple account of appointments or people may write down their deepest thoughts and feelings.

Georgia Nicolson is a typical teenager. In these extracts from her diary, she worries about going back to school.

Still Sunday, 11.35 a.m.
There are six things very wrong with my life:
1. I have one of those under-the-skin spots that will never come to a head but lurk in a red way for the next two years.
2. It is on my nose.
3. I have a three-year-old sister who may have peed somewhere in my room.
4. In fourteen days the summer hols will be over and then it will be back to Stalag 14 and Oberführer Frau Simpson and her bunch of sadistic 'teachers'.
5. I am very ugly and need to go into an ugly home.
6. I went to a party dressed as a stuffed olive.

Tuesday September 1st, 10.00 a.m.
Six days to school and counting. I wish my mum could be emancipated, a feminist, a working mother etc. and manage to do my ironing.

I thought I'd wear my pencil line skirt the first day back, with hold-up stockings and my ankle boots. I'm still not really resolved in the make-up department because if I do run into Hawkeye she'll make me take it off if she spots it. Then I'll get that shiny red face look which is so popular with PE teachers. On the other hand, I cannot possibly risk walking to school without make-up on. No matter how much I stick to the sidestreets, sooner or later I will be bound to bump into the Foxwood lads. The biggest worry of all is the bloody beret. I must consult with the gang to see what our plan is.

5.00 p.m.
We're having an emergency Beret and Other Forms of Torture meeting tomorrow at my place. I have got eyebrows now

Stalag 14 – German Prisoner of War Camp
Oberführer – Senior Leader, early paramilitary rank of the Nazi Party

(after shaving them off last week) but still look a bit on the startled earwig side.

Friday September 4th, 11.00 a.m.
... Jools said, 'Shall we talk beret plan?' At our stupid school you have to wear a beret with your outdoor uniform. It's a real pain because, as we know, everyone – and especially the French who invented it – looks like a stupid prat in a beret. And they flatten your hair. Last term we perfected a way of wearing it like a pancake. You flatten it out and then pin it with hair grips right at the back of your head. Still a pain, but you can't see it from the front. Ellen said she had made up a different method, called 'the sausage'. She showed us how to do it. She rolled her beret up really tight like a little sausage and then pinned it with hair grips right at the back in the centre of her head. You could hardly see it at all. It was brilliant. We decided to instigate Operation Sausage at the beginning of the term.

It has been a constant battle about these berets. The so-called grown-ups will not negotiate with us. We sent a deputation to the headmistress Slim (so-called because she weighs twenty-five stone... at least. Her feet cascade out of her shoes). At the deputation we asked why we had to wear berets. She said it was to keep standards up, and to enhance the image of the school in the community. I said, 'But the boys from Foxwood call out, "Have you got any onions?" I don't think they do respect us, I think they make a mock and a sham of us.'

Slim shook herself. It was a sort of habit she had when she was irritated with us (i.e. all the time). It made her look like jelly with shoes on.

'Georgia, you have had my last word on this, berets are to be worn to and from school. Why not think about something a bit more important, like perhaps getting less than twenty-one poor conduct marks next term?'

Oh, go on, play the old record again. Just because I am lively.

We did have another campaign last year, which was If You Want Us to Wear Our Berets, Let's Really Wear Our Berets. This involved the whole of our year pulling their berets right down over their heads with just their ears showing. It was very stunning, seeing one hundred girls at the

cascade – pour out   *deputation* – group of representatives

bus stop with just their ears showing. We stopped eventually (even though it really infuriated Slim and Hawkeye) because it was terribly hot and you couldn't see where you were going and it played havoc with your hair.

Monday September 7th, 8.30 a.m.
Overslept and had to race to get a lift to Jas's with my dad. No time for yoga or make-up. Oh well, I'll start tomorrow. God alone knows how the Dalai Lama copes on a daily basis. He must get up at dawn. Actually, I read somewhere that he does get up at dawn.

8.45 a.m.
Jas and I running like loonies up the hill to the school gate. I thought my head was going to explode I was so red, and I also just remembered I hadn't got my beret on. I could see Hawkeye at the school gate so no time for the sausage method. I just rammed it on my head. Bugger bugger, pant pant. As we ran up to the gate I catapulted into ... the Gorgeous God. He looked DIVINE in his uniform. He was with his mates, having a laugh and just strolling coolly along. He looked at me and said, 'You're keen.' I could have died.

9.00 a.m.
My only hope is that a) – he didn't recognise me and b) – if he did recognise me he likes the 'flushed, stupid idiot' look in a girl.

9.35 a.m.
After assembly I popped into the loos and looked in the mirror. Worst fears confirmed – I am Mrs Ugly. Small, swollen eyes, hair plastered to my skull, HUGE red nose. I look like a tomato in a school uniform. Well, that is that then.

4.00 p.m.
The bell. Thank God, now I can go home and kill myself.

7.00 p.m.
In bed. Uncle Eddie says there is an unseen force at work of which we have no comprehension... Well, if there is, why is it picking on me?

Dalai Lama – very wise Tibetan religious leader

1. In your own words, what does Georgia think is wrong with her life?

2. From the extract on Tuesday, September 1st, describe, in your own words, Georgia's main worries about returning to school.

3. Why do the girls hate the berets?

4. Why do the school authorities like the berets?

5. What happens on Georgia's first day? Does it all go according to plan?

6. What does Georgia think she looks like in her school uniform? Do you think she really looks this bad?

7. Why is Georgia embarrassed when she bumps into the 'Gorgeous God'?

8. How does Georgia feel after the first day at school?

9. Would you like to be friends with Georgia? Why or why not?

Make a list of the things that you like or dislike about what you wear to school.

OR

Starting in a new school can be a scary or exciting experience.

- Do you agree with this?
- What other words would you use to describe your first day?
- What are new students typically worried about?
- What are they looking forward to?

Write down your thoughts.

OR

Write a description of a typical morning from the moment your alarm clock rings to when you walk out of the door of your house.

In groups rewrite a piece from this diary, as if it was on Bebo or Twitter, from the point of view of the boy or Georgia. Pick someone to read it out to the class.

I Want to Live

Nina Lugovskaya

This is an extract from the diary of a thirteen-year-old Moscow schoolgirl. She lived in Russia at a time when the government was very strict. People could be sent to prison for no reason. She still worried about the same things as students all over the world, like exams and the never-ending wait for holidays.

18 April 1934

I can't wait for summer! That's all I want. Kolya and Granny call me a lazybones because I'm thinking about the holidays again. But they're wrong. You have to dream about something and want something.

I'm alone in the flat now. Mum's gone to see a friend and Dad's out, too. I'm getting on badly with him at the moment. Sometimes I just can't stand him and quite often I hate him. It's hideous when he suddenly starts hassling me. Yesterday, he and I had a row about something; he called me a fool and something else too and then pretty much every name under the sun. And I promised myself that I'd change the way we behaved towards each other, which has somehow become so unbearable. I decided to be less rude and stop being so sarcastic, but still not ask him for anything or be affectionate.

His petty tyranny drives me crazy. And I often thank God that I don't live in the eighteenth or nineteenth century, when the father of the family was the absolute lord and master. Life would be none too sweet for us under the rule of *my* highly esteemed parent. My antipathy towards Dad has grown so strong that sometimes I'd prefer if we had no father at all. At least then I'd be able to imagine him as kind and good.

18 May 1934

I'm sinking deeper and deeper into laziness and apathy. Yearning and boredom, the same as before. I really don't feel like doing my geography, but the exam's tomorrow. Mum asked me out for a walk, but I didn't go. I really didn't want to at all. What would I do with her and Dad? And Dad will start in with his painfully logical exhortations. Just recently, I simply can't stand him. Every word he says makes me angry. I make rude and caustic comments and, no matter how much I promise myself I'm going to behave better, it makes no difference.

That's part of the reason I'm so sick of everything: I can't stay at home, I feel I need to get as far away as I can. I'm not studying very much at all now, I hardly read anything. I'm bored and angry all the time, I feel I've been unlucky in life.

Tyranny – unjust use of authority
Antipathy – disgust
Apathy – lack of interest

Exhortations – urgent recommendations
Caustic – critical or sarcastic

1. Why do Nina's family call her a 'lazybones'?
2. What does Nina decide to do to improve her relationship with her father?
3. Why is she glad she doesn't live in the eighteenth or nineteenth century?
4. Why does Nina want to get as far away as she can?

5. Describe Nina's relationship with her father in your own words.
6. Why do you think Nina finds it so hard to study?

Imagine it is the week before one of the following:

- An important cup match
- Your first appearance on stage
- Your first day in a new school
- The school holidays
- Your first time on a plane

Write a series of three diary entries describing how you feel as you wait for the important event.

Sept 13th 2012

Capital Letters

Capital Letters are used:

- At the beginning of a sentence.
- For names of
  - people and places (*John, Helen, Cork, Ireland*)
  - book and film titles (*The Secret Garden, Spider-man*)
  - days and months (*Tuesday, January*)
  - brand names (*Nike, Supermac's*)

DIVE IN!

Rewrite the following sentences, putting in or removing **capital letters** where necessary.

1. KATIE AND JACK WENT TO GALWAY ON THEIR HOLIDAYS.

2. val and fiona really enjoyed reading dinosaurs, the new history book.

3. MY DENTAL APPOINTMENT IS ON WEDNESDAY THE FIFTEENTH OF APRIL.

4. we went to burger king for my birthday.

5. elvis presley only drank perrier water.

6. HAVE YOU SEEN MY LEVI JEANS?

7. the semi-final is on in athlone on 16 november.

8. WE HAD TO SEARCH ALL THE SHOPS: CLERYS, ARNOTTS, BROWN THOMAS AND THE STEPHEN'S GREEN CENTRE.

9. when i grow up, i'd like to be a firefighter, a nurse or a guard.

10. I THINK THE FUNNIEST AD ON TV AT THE MOMENT IS THE ONE FOR LYNX DEODORANT.

TAKE THE PLUNGE!

Correct the following passage, putting in capital letters wherever they are missing.

it was an exciting first half. the ballymore team were pleased with their performance, especially the great job done by their goalkeeper, seamus burke. it was ideal weather for the game. last monday it had rained for hours and hours. today the sun was shining. if they kept performing this well, the coach, terence o'brien, said that they would have a good chance of making the final in september. all they needed to do to improve was to read his famous book, everything i know about hurling.

WHY DON'T YOU...

- In a time limit of 60 seconds write as many sentences as you can. You cannot use lists of people or places.

- You must try to get as many capital letters into your sentences as possible, but they must be used correctly.

- When the teacher tells you the 60 seconds are up, put down your pen.

- Swap copies with the person next to you.

- For every capital letter you score one point, but for every mistake you lose a point.

Full Stops

Full Stops are used:

- To mark the end of a sentence, e.g. 'This is the end of my sentence.'

- After initials, e.g. M. Mouse, G. Ryan, J. Roberts.

- For abbreviations, e.g. Prof. (Professor), Wed. (Wednesday), Sq. (Square), if the abbreviation does not end on the same letter as the full word. For Mr, for example, we do not use a full stop as the abbreviation ends on the same letter as the full word.

- To let the reader know that you should take a long breath because you are at the end of a sentence.

DIVE IN!

Re-write the following sentences using the necessary **full stops** and **capital letters.**

1. mary and niall went to waterford to see the college facilities at wit

2. I would like to walk down park ave in new york during the winter

3. st jude is the patron saint of hopeless cases

4. dr dre and eminem are in talks with emi records

5. hollywood in the usa is the home of tv programmes like the simpsons, american idol and desperate housewives

TAKE THE PLUNGE!

Rewrite the following passage, writing out all the **abbreviations** fully and putting in the necessary **capital letters.** Remember the rules of punctuation!

prof. james mitchell has made a special study of secret societies in co. wexford. last fri., the fifteenth of dec., his new book was launched at hopkin's bookstore on parnell sq. in attendance was mr martin cullen td and an rté camera crew. a party was later held at the gaa headquarters in croke park.

- Divide the class into two opposing teams, A and B. There is no need to move. Your teacher will divide the blackboard into two sides, A and B.

- On your own, try to punctuate the passage on the right.

- When you think you have finished punctuating the passage, put your hand in the air and your teacher will call you to the board to write out the passage correctly.

- If you make a mistake, you will have to sit down and someone else from your team must put their hand up to be chosen to continue from the point where you made a mistake. When the board is full, it can be cleaned, and the team member can continue writing.

- The team that completes the passage on the board first wins.

he put his bag down on a chair in the hall.and followed me into harry's room he was wearing bedroom slippers and he walked across the floor noiselessly. delicately, like a careful cat harry watched him out of the sides of his eyes. when dr ganderbai reached the bed he looked down at harry and smiled. confident and reassuring, nodding his head to tell harry it was a simple matter and he was not to worry but just to leave it to dr ganderbai.then he turned and went back to the hall and i followed him we went into the kitchen and he sterilized a needle.he picked up a bag and together we returned to the room harry's eyes were bright now and wide open.ganderbai bent over harry and very cautiously, like a man handling sixteenth century lace, he rolled up the pyjamas sleeve to the elbow without moving the arm i noticed he stood well away from the bed. Ⓡ

Witch Child

Celia Rees

It is the seventeenth century, Mary's grandmother has been accused of witchcraft. The punishment is hanging. Mary's diary describes the day of the hanging.

It is a cold day, even for early spring. White frost on the ground and green barely touching the trees, but folk come from far and near for the hanging. They crowd the market square worse than Mop Day.

It is dangerous for me to be there. I see them glancing and whispering, 'That's her, the grand-daughter', 'daughter of the Devil, more like', then they turn away, sniggering, hands covering their mouths, faces turning red at the lewd images they conjure in their own mind's eye. The evil is in themselves.

I should flee, get away. They will turn on me next unless I go. But where to? What am I to do? Get lost. Die in the forest. I look around. Eyes, hard with hatred, slide from mine. Mouths twitch between leering and sneering. I will not run away into the forest because that is what they want me to do.

I keep my eyes forward now, staring at the gallows. They have hammered away for a night and a day putting it up. You can smell the fresh cut wood even where I am at the back of the crowd.

What powers do they think we have, my grandmother and I? If she had any real power, would she not be able to undo the locks to their stinking dungeon and fly through the air to safety? Would she not call up her master, Satan, to blast and shrivel them to dust and powder? And if I had any powers, any at all, I would destroy them all, right here and now. I would turn them into a mass of toads. I would turn them into leprous blind newts and set them to eat themselves. I would cover their bodies with suppurating plague sores. I would curse them from generation to generation, down through the ages, so their children and their children's children bore gaggling half-wits. I would addle their heads, curdling, corrupting the insides of their skulls until their brains dripped from their noses like bloody mucus …

I was so lost in my curses that only the sudden silence of the crowd brought me back to what was about to happen. Black figures stood on

Mop Day – a hiring fair

lewd – rude

leering – staring slyly and meanly

suppurating – leaking pus

addle – confuse

curdling – thickening

the pale boards, silhouetted against the white of the sky: Witchfinder, Minister, Hangman. In the unexpected quiet, a sneeze sounded loud. Obadiah Wilson's thin figure bent forward, suddenly convulsed. He took a handkerchief from his pocket and held it to his face as sneeze after sneeze racked him. When he took it away the crowd drew breath, blood bloomed thick and red on the snow white linen. It was the only colour on the whole platform.

My grandmother was brought forward for all the crowd to see. She was held, arms pinioned behind her, and pushed to the foot of the ladder which leant against the gallows tree. She ignored the eyes on her, looking over the upturned heads, searching for me. Her eyes found mine and she smiled. Her glance went sideways to Obadiah Wilson, self-appointed Witchfinder, trying to staunch the blood pouring from his nostrils and she nodded very slightly as if to say 'well done.' She nodded again to someone behind me.

That was the last I saw of her. The hangman stepped forward, hood raised to cover her face, and at the same time a cloak closed around me. I was taken down one of the steep alleys leading from the market and was stepping into a waiting carriage when I heard the crowds roar.

silhouetted – outlined against the light

pinioned – held fast

staunch – stop the flow

1. How do the people react to Mary?
2. What does Mary think would happen if she ran away?
3. What would Mary do if she had any power?
4. Who are the three people standing on the gallows?
5. Why doesn't she see the actual hanging?

Read the next two pages and then try the following questions:

6. When do you realise that Mary herself may be a witch? **P Q E**

7. Would you like to read more of this story? Give reasons for your answer. **P Q E**

From now on you will be expected to write more detailed answers to English questions. For example, if you were asked,

Does Mary believe that her grandmother is a witch? How do you know?

you should answer using the following method.

You begin your answer using the words from the question to make your main

Mary does not believe that her grandmother is a witch because she cannot escape.

Then you must use evidence directly from the extract to prove your point.

This is called a

Mary says, 'If she had real power, would she not be able to undo the locks to their stinking dungeon and fly through the air to safety?'

Remember to use 'inverted commas' when you quote from the story.

Lastly, you must   how this quote proves your point.

We know that Mary does not believe that her grandmother is a witch because she does not have the power to free herself.

So your answer should look like this:

Mary does not believe that her grandmother is a witch because she cannot escape. Mary says, 'If she had real power, would she not be able to undo the locks to their stinking dungeon and fly through the air to safety?' We know that Mary does not believe that her grandmother is a witch because she does not have the power to free herself.

From now on you will see this code next to many questions: **PQE**. This is to remind you to use the **PQE** method.

Invisible City

M. G. Harris

Nowadays people keep diaries in a different way. Bloggers write about their lives, thoughts and feelings online.

http://www.thejoshuafiles.co.uk

YOU HAVE WANDERED INTO A CONSPIRACY-THEORY ZONE

This blog belongs to:
Josh Garcia

What's it all about?
This is a record of my search for the truth behind my father's death.

Age:
Thirteen

Location:
Oxford, U.K.

About me:
Me, I'm the son of a Mexican archaeologist (Dad) and a British history teacher (Mum).

Favourite bands:
Green Day, Arctic Monkeys, Nirvana

Favourite books:
His Dark Materials

Favourite sports:
Capoeira – it's a Brazilian martial art. Erm … that's about it!

If eight out of ten cat owners prefer M&Ms, what do the other two like?
They live on a pure diet of orange Smarties.

BLOG ENTRY: WALKING CONTRADICTION

I need a place where I can get rid of all these things going on in my head. Things you don't want to talk about. Things your friends, your family don't want you to talk about.

Hence this blog.

I didn't use to be like this, mooching around on my own, writing down my deepest, darkest thoughts. It wasn't even that long ago that it happened – a couple of weeks back, I was just another guy at school. OK, probably not the cleverest or strongest, definitely not the best-looking or most popular, but apart from that I don't think I had a single complaint in the world.

The thing was, I didn't know it. I thought my problems were a big deal.

Well … I had no idea.

There was this phone call and people are telling me I need to go home early. So I'm on my skateboard and down the road.

Never thinking it through. Never guessing that somewhere up the street, a storm was brewing. I sailed towards it, practically singing.

Innocent.

Stupid.

1. Who does this blog belong to and what is it recording?

2. What did you learn about the writer of this blog?

3. What does the writer say he was like before he started this blog? **P Q E**

4. Why do you think he is writing a blog and not talking to his friends?

5. Would you like to read any more of this blog? Why or why not? **P Q E**

Write a blog entry about yourself using the headings in the extract above. Feel free to add new headings if you want to tell people more about yourself! **R**

OR

Write an e-mail to Joshua giving your opinion of his blog.

In groups, answer the following questions and report back to the class.

● Do you have a Bebo page? Why or why not?

● What are the good things about Bebo and other social networking sites?

● What are the negative things?

● Should Bebo be accessible in school?

● How long do you spend online every day?

● What advice would you give to someone who has never used Bebo?

Careful With Commas!

Commas

Read this sentence:

Woman, without her man, is nothing.
What do you think this sentence is saying?

Now read it again:

Woman, without her, man is nothing.
Do you think that this sentence has a different meaning? What makes the difference?

Commas are used:

- To mark a short pause in the sentence, e.g. 'Polluting our seas is not just foolish, it is also dangerous.'

- Between words in a list replacing 'and'. Instead of saying, 'Hurling and gymnastics and tennis are all enjoyable sports' you can say, 'Hurling, gymnastics and tennis are all enjoyable sports.' *Notice there is no comma in front of the 'and'.*

Rewrite these sentences, putting **commas** in the correct places.

1. The skills needed for mountaineering are stamina strength determination and a head for heights.

2. Whether he is guilty or not is irrelevant justice is the important issue.

3. I was on the beach running with my dog when my lace opened and I fell.

4. The new Nissan Primo has four-wheel drive anti-lock braking system central locking and a sporty exterior.

5. The weather forecast for tomorrow is showers in the east so make sure you bring along your umbrellas.

Rewrite this passage, putting **commas** in where you think they are needed.

The azure blue sea sparkled in the summer sun. Jumping from rock to rock I paused glancing around the bay thinking about the events that had brought me here. It was hard to believe that a few short days ago I was stuck in a damp dark dingy classroom listening to the dull dreary drone of the teacher's voice. I took a deep breath savouring the sea air I still couldn't believe it here I was in the Seychelles.

Commas are normally used to tell you to pause and take a short breath but …

Have a competition to see who can survive this comma-less sentence. If you have a watch with a timer you could use it. As soon as the person draws breath or stumbles over a word they are out.

The fascinating witches who put the scintillating stitches in the britches of the boys who put the powder on the noses of the faces of the ladies of the harem of the court of King Caractacus were just passing by the boys who put the powder on the noses of the faces of the ladies of the harem of the court of King Caractacus were just passing by but if you want to take a picture of the fascinating witches who put the scintillating stitches in the britches of the boys who put the powder on the noses of the faces of the ladies of the harem of the court of King Caractacus you're too late because they've just passed by.

Letter to a Friend

Personal letters are what you write when your mobile phone is broken, or the e-mail is down!

Your address and the date

Greeting

Start a new paragraph for a new topic; don't forget to indent

22, Green St,
Westport,
Co. Mayo.
5th September 2011

Dear Paul,

I am gutted to be back in school. Wish it was the holidays again. Only another three boring months until Christmas!

Remember the day we went to the beach and Josie wore the seaweed as a wig? I swear my biology teacher is doing the same thing! You should see the state of her!

Has your Irish improved since Irish college? You'd think with all that work I could do better than a 'D' in my first test. I'm determined to do better this year – serious exams on the way!

By the way, did you ever get your mobile phone back from Mr McCarthy? Some cheek confiscating it, just 'cos you were texting at three a.m. I think you should just have had to pay a fine.

I suppose you're not in touch with any of the gang. Nobody but a saddo like me would be bothered to write you a letter. You'd better write back, or at least text me! Gotta go, the joys of homework await!

All the best,
Jack.

Signature

WHY DON'T YOU...

Write a letter to a friend about:

- A recent holiday
- Something that has upset you or made you happy
- Your birthday
- Your new school
- A funny incident

Ice Man – The Remarkable Adventures of Antarctic Explorer Tom Crean

Michael Smith

- A biography is the story of a person's life written by somebody else.
- An autobiography is the story of a person's life, told by the person themselves.
- A memoir is a book written about a part of a person's life.

Tom Crean, a Kerryman, was an Antarctic explorer. He was a member of Ernest Shackleton's crew which left England in 1914 with the intention of crossing Antarctica. However, after sailing for five months, their ship, Endurance, *became trapped in ice. Nine months later, the ship was crushed by the ice and had to be abandoned. The expedition members camped on the ice floes for five more months. With a deadly Antarctic winter closing in, they were forced to take to their lifeboats to seek land. After five desperate days they landed on the rocky Elephant Island, but there was no hope of rescue from there, as the island was completely isolated. Therefore, six men, including Crean, had to take to sea in a tiny open lifeboat called the* James Caird. *They adapted the lifeboat by adding a mast and canvas sails and by covering the open seats with canvas decking. They then had to take this makeshift sailboat 1200 km across the stormy Southern Ocean in an attempt to reach the only inhabited island, South Georgia. They left 22 men waiting for rescue on Elephant Island. Everyone knew they had very little hope of success …*

But the toughest job on board the *James Caird* was navigating the vessel to the island. This task fell to Captain Frank Worsley, the captain of the *Endurance*, who was known as Skipper.

Even a small margin of error in the Skipper's navigation would send the *James Caird* sailing past the little island and out into the South Atlantic Ocean – the countless kilometres of open water between the continents of Africa and South America.

If the *Caird* missed South Georgia there was no way of fighting back to land against the strong currents. Skipper had only one chance to find the island. But the boat's safety was threatened by different dangers.

Dawn broke one morning to find thick ice had formed on the *Caird*'s canvas decking during the cold night. Sea spray froze as soon as it splashed across the deck. By morning the ice was 15 cm (6 inches) thick and threatened to capsize the boat under its weight.

Urgent action was needed and Tom bravely volunteered to crawl out along the canvas decking to chip away at the ice. As he crawled along on his stomach, the boat rolled heavily and he was almost thrown into the water.

Tom clung to the decking with one hand and knocked off the ice with the other. But he could only hang on for a short while in the freezing temperatures and other members of the crew inched forward and took his place.

It was a thankless task. No sooner had they chipped away at the ice than fresh spray splashed over the deck and immediately froze on the canvas once more.

It was a constant battle and the men risked their lives by crawling out onto the deck to break off the ice. Luckily, their efforts worked and the *Caird* had survived a terrible fright.

Another crisis arose soon after. In the distance someone noticed a white cloud low on the horizon and they thought the sky was brightening.

Suddenly, it was noticed that the bright cloud was moving towards them. It was a giant wave.

'For God's sake, hold on,' someone shouted.

The *James Caird* was catapulted forward and almost lifted bodily out of the sea as the giant wave crashed down on the vessel. The men were thrown to the floor and the water engulfed them. The men were so wet that for a moment, it was not clear whether the boat was still upright.

But the giant wave disappeared as quickly as it came. The *James Caird* had survived, somehow.

Vast amounts of water had poured into the little boat and it was again threatened with capsizing. The men grabbed the nearest containers and bailed for their lives. It took an hour of frantic work and once again the *Caird* had a narrow escape. In the commotion no one noticed that the sea had broken into the precious barrel of drinking water. It was badly fouled by the salty sea water.

The hungry, tired and soaked crew of the *Caird* now faced perhaps the worst torture of all – thirst.

Apart from making drinks, they could not cook the hoosh without water. It meant gnawing on raw, dry rations.

Tom tried to filter the brackish water through cloth, but it still tasted horribly salty and made them feel even more thirsty. As days passed, their thirst grew worse. Their lips cracked and tongues were swollen. The situation was desperate.

In spite of this, the *James Caird* was defying the odds and making good progress towards South Georgia. Winds, although very strong, were mostly in their favour and pushing the craft on the correct course to the island.

After two weeks, the Skipper calculated they must be near their goal. But the island was nowhere to be seen.

DIVE IN!

1. Why did the six men undertake such a dangerous journey?

2. What would happen if Worsley made a mistake?

3. What dangers were created by the freezing temperatures?

4. What did they think the wave was?

5. What was the lasting damage that the wave caused which made life more difficult for the men?

TAKE THE PLUNGE!

6. What sort of a person do you think Tom Crean was, based on the evidence from this extract? **P Q E**

7. What did you think of the description of the men's thirst?

8. List the various obstacles that the men had to overcome.

WHY DON'T YOU...

Finish this story. You must decide:

● Whether the men find the island or not

● How many of the men survive

● If they make it back to Elephant Island to rescue the 22 men left behind

OR

Choose a person, living or dead, famous or not, and write a short biographical piece about them. You may need to do some extra research, such as interviews, if the person is living and local, a library visit or web searches.

Tom Crean

THRASH IT OUT!

Imagine your class is the exploration team and you are stranded on Elephant Island. The crew is divided into the following groups:

● Ship's Officers (who can navigate)
● Engineers (who look after a ship's engines)
● Able Seamen (ordinary sailors)
● Surgeons
● Cook/Waiter

● Scientists (who document scientific discoveries on the journey)
● Artist/Photographer (they record the exploration)
● Firemen (who shovel coal into a ship's engines)

Your teacher will assign you a role. Only six of you can go into the lifeboat. Make an argument to the class to convince them to allow you to go. Have a class vote at the end to see which six succeed in escaping Elephant Island. **R**

Know Your Nouns

A **Noun** is the name of a person, place or thing.

There are four types of nouns.

A **Common Noun** is any ordinary object (sun, table, glass).

A **Proper Noun** is a specifically named object like a person (*J*ane), a place (*F*rance), a day (*C*hristmas *D*ay), a month (*A*ugust) or a brand name (*N*ike). All proper nouns get capital letters.

An **Abstract Noun** is the name of a quality or emotion (love, bravery, beauty).

A **Collective Noun** is a name for a group of similar objects that form a whole (a **gaggle** of geese, a **crowd** of people, an **audience** of spectators, a **herd** of cattle).

DIVE IN!

Draw four columns in your copybook with the headings 'Common', 'Proper', 'Abstract' and 'Collective'. Put the following **nouns** into the correct columns.

sofa	doctor	Tuesday
humour	crowd	pilot
table	dog	diamond
squad	flour	Ireland
pack	bottle	James
love	horse	band
flock	crate	youth
sympathy	library	iron
music	blanket	Cork
duck	Adidas	set
wisdom	Easter	fire
pity	car	litter
Chicago	coffee	madness
night	Sam	pen

TAKE THE PLUNGE!

1. Complete the following word puzzle, using **common nouns.** Choose the words that fit into the empty spaces and write them into your copybook.

morning, airport, hands, sun, friend, planes.

This _____ the _____ was shining here in Africa. He walked through the _____ listening to the _____ take off outside. When he got to 'Arrivals', he looked around for his _____, Samuel. He spotted him eventually, and the two men shook _____.

2. Rewrite the following passage into your copybook and underline any abstract nouns that you can find.

The wisdom of the old man was apparent in the deep understanding of his twinkling eyes. His face contained no beauty, but it was full of love and compassion. This made it easier to talk to him, and Jake felt a wave of friendship towards him. He listened with empathy to the boy's story, and then began to speak …

24

TAKE THE PLUNGE!

3. In your copybook, write the **collective noun** used for a group of these objects.

- A _____ of lions
- A _____ of buffalo
- A _____ of flowers
- A _____ of bees
- A _____ of ships
- A _____ of cutlery
- A _____ of drawers
- A _____ of trees
- A _____ of mountains
- A _____ of flats

WHY DON'T YOU...

Pick one of the words below as a starting point. The teacher will begin by saying that word. The next person must say another word, connected to it, but it must be a **noun** (e.g. the first person might say 'mountain', the next person 'rock', the next 'concert', and so on). Begin at the top of the room, and go through the class in succession. You may not hesitate or stumble over the word: if you do, you are out. If you use a word that is not a noun, you are out. If you repeat a word that has already been used, you are out.

The last person left is the winner!

BELL   WATER   TELEVISION

MONEY   SCHOOL

Pronouns

A **Pronoun** is used instead of a noun in a sentence.

There are three types of pronouns:

Personal Pronouns are used when you speak about yourself or another person, e.g. I, you, they.

Write a list of the **personal pronouns** that you can find in these sentences.

1. Claire was delighted with her new fireplace.

2. When Kevin was finished with the DVD, he brought it back to the shop.

3. I had a great dream last night.

4. I don't like football, but he loves it.

5. 'I don't fancy her,' Brian said, 'she's not my type!'

6. Make yourself at home while I call them in from the garden.

7. David and Stephen both wanted the last slice of cake, so they fought over it.

8. 'I'm delighted with you,' she said, 'you have done us proud.'

Possessive Pronouns indicate the owner of something, e.g. 'It's my ice-cream' could be replaced by 'It's *mine*'.

Rewrite this passage into your copybook, filling in the missing **possessive pronouns.**

theirs, yours, mine, ours, mine, hers, mine

Coming home from the cinema I checked my bag. Because it was _____ I expected to see my phone, but instead I found Tony's phone. I held up the phone and said, 'Who owns this?' Tony said, 'That's _____,' but then Melissa claimed that it was _____.' Well,' I asked, 'is it _____? Or is it Tony's?' They smiled at me and together they said, 'It's _____, we bought it together last week!' I was relieved it was _____, but I still don't know where _____ is.

Relative Pronouns tell us more about the nouns in the sentence, e.g. 'The man who bought a new car just walked by.' Here we learn something more about the man, which is that he has bought a new car. 'That's the beach where I nearly drowned.' Here we find out something more about a beach – that the person nearly drowned on it.

The five most important relative pronouns are who, which, where, whose and that.

Pick out the **relative pronouns** in this passage.

The girl who was my best friend in primary school went to a different secondary school, where she made new friends. These girls were the type that mocked others, something which my friend had never previously done. One day she borrowed my bag for school but when her new friends found out whose bag it was, they threw it in the river. She said she was sorry but that will not bring back my bag.

Chinese Cinderella

Adeline Yen Mah

Adeline Yen Mah grew up in China as the youngest daughter in a large family. She had a very lonely childhood, and her only friend was a little duckling that she named 'PLT' for Precious Little Treasure. The family also had a vicious dog called Jackie. On this occasion, her father decides to test whether Jackie's new obedience lessons are working.

'Since it's so hot tonight,' Father suggested, 'why don't we all cool off in the garden after dinner? It will also give us a chance to test Jackie's obedience.' He turned to Big Brother. 'Go fetch one of those ducklings that the Huangs brought. We'll have some fun tonight!'

There was a momentary silence. To us children, Father's announcement was like a death sentence. Immediately, I had a picture in my mind of my pet being torn to pieces between Jackie's frothing, ravenous jaws. I felt as if my heart had stopped beating. I held myself rigid, in a world full of dread, knowing with absolute certainty that the doomed duckling would be mine.

Big Brother scraped back his chair, ran upstairs and came down with PLT. Everyone avoided looking at me. Even Aunt Baba could not bear to meet my eyes. Father strode into the garden with PLT on his palm and sat down on a lounge chair, flanked by all the grown-ups. We children sprawled in a semi-circle on the grass. Jackie greeted his master joyfully, wagging his tail and jumping up and down with happiness.

Father released PLT and placed her in the centre of the lawn. My little pet appeared bewildered by all the commotion. She stood quite still for a few moments, trying to get her bearings: a small, yellow, defenceless creature beset with perils, surrounded by humans wanting to test their dog in a gamble with her life. I sat stiffly with downcast eyes. For a moment, I was unable to focus properly. 'Don't move, PLT! Please don't move!' I prayed silently. 'As long as you keep still, you have a chance!'

Jackie was ordered to 'sit' about two metres away. He sat on his hind legs with his large tongue hanging out, panting away. His fierce eyes were riveted on his prey. Father kept two fingers on his collar while the German Shepherd fidgeted and strained restlessly.

ravenous — starving

beset — surrounded

riveted — firmly fixed

The tension seemed palpable while I hoped against hope that fate could be side-stepped in some way. Then PLT cocked her head in that achingly familiar way of hers and spotted me. Chirping happily, she waddled unsteadily towards me. Tempted beyond endurance, Jackie sprang forward. In one powerful leap, he broke away from Father's restraint and pounced on PLT, who looked up at me pleadingly as if I was supposed to have an answer to all her terror.

palpable – could almost be touched

Father dashed over, enraged by Jackie's defiance. Immediately, Jackie released the bird from his jaws, but with a pang I saw PLT's left leg dangling lifelessly and her tiny webbed foot twisted at a grotesque angle. Blood spurted briskly from an open wound.

grotesque – awkward and unnatural

I was overwhelmed with horror. My whole world turned desolate. I ran over without a word, cradled PLT tenderly in my arms and carried her upstairs. Placing her on my bed, I wrapped my mortally wounded pet in my best school scarf and lay down next to her. It was a night of grief I have never forgotten.

DIVE IN!

1. How did Adeline feel when her father told her brother to fetch one of the ducklings?

2. How did the rest of her family react when they realised it was her precious duckling?

3. Why was the duckling bewildered?

4. Describe briefly, in your own words, what happened.

TAKE THE PLUNGE!

5. What words helped you to picture the duckling?
P Q E

6. What kind of a man do you think Adeline's father was?
P Q E

7. How did the ending of the story make you feel?

WHY DON'T YOU...

Write a description of a pet you have, or have had in the past. Think about your pet's personality, as well as how it looks. Did it ever get you into trouble, or rescue you? How do you feel about your pet?

OR

Write an incident from the autobiography of your pet (real or imaginary).

THRASH IT OUT!

Do you think that animal testing should be allowed? Have a class discussion on this issue, and write out the main points of the discussion at home.

29

Vexed About Verbs?

A Verb is an action word. Every sentence must contain a verb.

I **ran** a great race.
I **thought** about the problem.
John **is** a happy boy.
Brian **works** in a shop.
Jane could **see** the monster.

Put the following **verbs** into sentences.

is	laughs	swimming
running	speaking	crying
cleaned	think	taught
jump	watched	sob
giggles	remembered	joked

Place a brush at the top of the classroom. Normally you 'sweep' with a brush, but for this game you must pretend the brush is some other object. For example it could be a snooker cue and you could mime 'playing snooker' with it. Go to the top of the class one by one and mime an action with the brush. Write a list of the verbs that you see mimed. Write a story for homework incorporating some of these verbs.

Pick out the **verbs** from the following passage.

Big Brother scraped back his chair, ran upstairs and came down with PLT. Everyone avoided looking at me. Even Aunt Baba could not bear to meet my eyes. Father strode into the garden with PLT on his palm and sat down on a lounge chair, flanked by all the grown-ups. We children sprawled in a semi-circle on the grass. Jackie greeted his master joyfully, wagging his tail and jumping up and down with happiness.

Adverbs

An Adverb tells you more about the action.

I **swiftly** ran a great race.
I thought **carefully** about the problem.
John is a **really** happy boy.
Brian works **diligently** in a shop.
Jane could **barely** see the monster.

Think of **adverbs** to describe these verbs, and put them in sentences.

run	laugh	swim
clean	speak	cry
jump	think	taught
giggle	watch	sob
is	joke	remember

Write out the sentences below into your copybook, using the following **adverbs**.

cheerily precisely hungrily boldly

sadly angrily defiantly shyly

1. Paul _____ stood up to the bully.

2. Margaret _____ introduced herself to the group.

3. Sarah entered the room, crying _____ as she did so.

4. Somewhere in the castle I could hear someone whistling _____.

5. The wolves howled _____ in the darkness.

6. The surgeon cut _____ into the brain tumour.

7. 'To _____ go where no man has gone before', is the *Star Trek* motto.

8. The door was slammed _____ after the argument.

Think about the different ways people do things, even something as simple as eating their food. Look at the list of food and **adverbs** below, and choose one from each. Then, when the teacher asks you, mime eating your food in the manner chosen. The class must guess the food and the adverb.

spaghetti	reluctantly
oysters	hungrily
cod liver oil	fussily
a chicken wing	ravenously
crisps	distastefully
candy floss	slowly
a HUGE sandwich	greedily
a chilli pepper	nervously
hot soup	secretly
an ice-cream cone	painfully
a worm	messily

Fever Pitch

Nick Hornby

Nick Hornby is obsessed with soccer. Here he describes some of the bizarre things he does to bring his team good luck. He supports Arsenal and Cambridge United (quite a small team). Fever Pitch *is the title of his memoir about his life as a football fan.*

What happened was, Chris Roberts bought a sugar mouse from Jack Reynolds ('The Rock King'), bit its head off, dropped it in the Newmarket Road before he could get started on the body, and it got run over by a car. And that afternoon Cambridge United, who had hitherto been finding life difficult in the Second Division (two wins all season, one home, one away), beat Orient 3–1, and a ritual was born. Before each home game we, all of us, trooped into the sweet shop, purchased our mice, walked outside, bit the head off as though we were removing the pin from a grenade, and tossed the torsos under the wheels of oncoming cars; Jack Reynolds would stand in the doorway watching us, shaking his head sorrowfully. United, thus protected, remained unbeaten at the Abbey for months.

I know that I am particularly stupid about rituals, and have been ever since I started going to football matches, and I know also that I am not alone. I can remember when I was young having to take with me to Highbury a piece of putty, or blu-tack, or some stupid thing, which I pulled on nervously all afternoon; I can also remember having to buy a programme from the same programme seller, and having to enter the stadium through the same turnstile.

There have been hundreds of similar bits of nonsense, all designed to guarantee victories for one or other of my two teams. During Arsenal's protracted and nerve-racking semi-final campaign against Liverpool in 1980, I turned the radio off half-way through the second half of the last game; Arsenal were winning 1–0, and as Liverpool had equalised in the last seconds of the previous game, I couldn't bear to hear it through to the end. I played a Buzzcocks album instead (the *Singles – Going Steady* compilation album), knowing that side one would take me through to the final whistle. We won the match, and I insisted that my flatmate, who worked in a record store, should play the album at twenty past four

on Cup Final afternoon, although it did no good. (I have my suspicions that he might have forgotten.)

I have tried eating cheese-and-onion crisps at a certain point in the first half; I have tried not setting the video for live games (the team seems to have suffered badly in the past when I have taped the matches in order to study the performance when I get home); I have tried lucky socks, and lucky shirts, and lucky hats, and lucky friends, and have attempted to exclude others who I feel bring with them nothing but trouble for the team.

Nothing (apart from the sugar mice) has ever been any good. But what else can we do when we're so *weak?*

hitherto –
up to then

rituals –
an action often repeated,
with great importance
attached to it

protracted –
long, drawn out

1. What is the ritual for Cambridge United matches?

2. What other rituals does Nick Hornby have?

3. What happened during the 1980 Liverpool–Arsenal match?

4. Which ritual did you think was the most ridiculous?

5. How can you tell that Nick Hornby is a football fanatic? **P Q E**

6. Do you think he really believes in his rituals?

7. Do you have any superstitions that you believe bring you luck when you need it?

Write a television or radio commentary for a sporting occasion of your choice, as if you were live on air. Try to capture the excitement and the tension of a particular moment.

OR

Choose your favourite sport and write a paragraph describing an event. Look at the **Brainstorm** on the next page for help. **R**

OR

Write a letter from Nick Hornby to a friend of his telling him about a football match he has been to, which was either really wonderful or really awful.

Writing Paragraphs

Before you write a paragraph it helps if you brainstorm. This means scribbling down all your ideas roughly before you write. It can be done in one or two minutes. Look at the example below about a cross-country race.

Brainstorm

When you do a paragraph brainstorm like this for your chosen sport, use the following steps:

- Think about **nouns** to begin with (the words in **black** below)

- Change pen colour and put in some **adjectives** (the words in **red** below)

- Change pen colour again and add in **verbs** and **adverbs** (the words in **blue**)

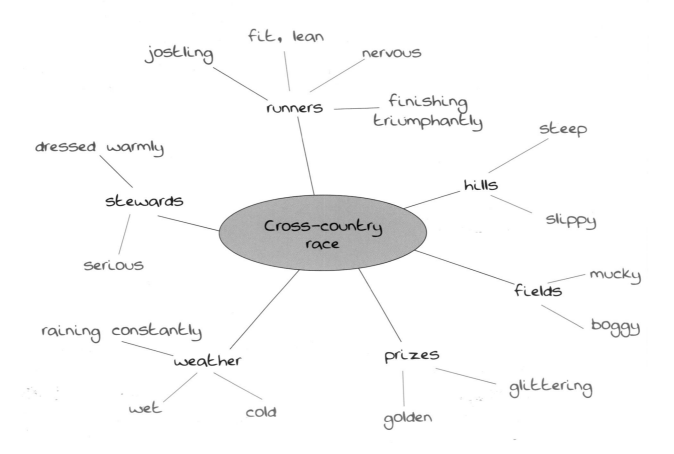

jostling

fit, lean

nervous

runners

finishing triumphantly

steep

hills

slippy

dressed warmly

stewards

Cross-country race

serious

mucky

fields

boggy

raining constantly

weather

prizes

glittering

wet

cold

golden

Serious Sentences!

You can't write well unless you understand the structure of a sentence. A sentence begins with a capital letter and ends with a full stop. It must make complete sense on its own. Look at this sentence:

Dog bites man.

This sentence is made up of two nouns, 'Dog' and 'man', and a verb, 'bites'.

Now look at this sentence:

Man bites dog.

Here you have the exact same nouns and verb but with a completely different meaning because the order of the words has been changed.

Every sentence must have a **verb,** e.g. 'bites'. This is also called the **predicate.**

The thing doing the action is called the **subject.** In the first sentence, the dog is the **subject** because it is biting, *but* in the second sentence, the man is the **subject** because he is biting.

The thing to which the action is being done is called the **object.** In the first sentence, the man is the **object** because he is bitten, *but* in the second sentence, the dog is the **object** because it is bitten!

Here are a few more examples:

The girl	wore	the uniform.
subject	predicate	object
The ball	bounced	on the path.
subject	predicate	object
The film	frightened	the children.
subject	predicate	object

Draw three columns in your copybook and divide these sentences into **subject, predicate** and **object.**

1. The class waited for the teacher.
2. The wind blew down the tree.
3. Paula waved to her boyfriend.
4. The cow ate the grass.
5. I am sitting on the chair.

Remember, no matter how long or short your sentence is, there should always be a subject and a verb (predicate).

The Secret World of the Irish Male

Joseph O'Connor

What does Valentine's Day really mean? I'm thinking of the exuberant canter down to the letterbox on the morning of February 14th, the blood scuttling through the veins at top speed, the tongue flapping with anticipation, the nerves doing gymnastics, the exquisite agony of it all, only to be followed by disappointment, the bare doormat, the poignantly cardless climb back up to the scratcher, the placing of the head beneath the duvet, the agonized screeching of abusive epithets and the subsequent moistening of the pillowcase with tears so salty you could sprinkle them on chips. Calling one's child Valentine would be like calling it Disappointment. And Disappointment O'Connor would not be much of a name for a child, even though, no doubt, it would eventually get abbreviated to Dizzy O'Connor – and I've met one or two of those in my time, God only knows. Sappy O'Connor would be another possibility, I suppose.

When I was six I had a teacher called Miss Glennon. She was a very good teacher. She believed that there was more to early education than the repetitive chanting of ideologically suspect nursery rhymes and the digital manipulation of plasticine, and so, when Valentine's Day came around one year, she made every boy and girl in the class write a Valentine card, complete with a poem. For those less creatively gifted students, Miss Glennon explained that it was acceptable to start off with the time-honoured couplet 'roses are red, violets are blue'. We got ten minutes. The completed cards were then placed in two piles at the top of the class, one for boys and one for girls. We each had to pick one at random, and read it aloud to the assembled unwashed.

At the time, I entertained an uneasy but quite fervent affection for Michele Killen, a tempestuous redhead who could play conkers like nobody's business, and whose pipe-cleaner men were the talk of Saint Joseph of Cluny School. Michele did not like me much. On one occasion she called me 'weird', I recall, but, hey, it was kind of a Burton and Taylor thing. The card I picked out, however, came from a girl called Sheena whose hand I always had to hold whenever Miss Glennon took us on nature walks, which was a little too often for

exuberant – very energetic

exquisite – sharp

poignantly – bittersweetly

epithets – curses

abbreviated – shortened

digital manipulation – working with fingers

fervent – strongly felt, passionate

Burton and Taylor – famous movie stars who loved each other but fought constantly

incontinent –
uncontrollable
flow

my liking. All I remember about Sheena is that she had a perpetually runny nose. The contents of her incontinent nostrils ebbed and flowed like the proud majestic Shannon, and the hand which she used to wipe said nostrils was also, invariably, the hand which she used to hold my own as tightly as she could. My own hand, that is. Not my own nostrils. But anyway. Me and Sheena were frequently stuck together by something more than just love.

Flushed with romantic excitement, I stood up at the top of the class that morning long ago and began to read out the words Sheena had written. They were, and here I quote in full, 'Roses are red, Violets are blue, I think you're horrible and you are like poo.' I was shattered. Not only was the thought less than affectionate, but I mean, it didn't even bloody scan properly.

1. Why was Valentine's Day so exciting? What always happened?

2. What did Miss Glennon ask the class to do?

3. Who did Joseph O'Connor secretly fancy and what were her special talents?

4. Who did Joseph not like and why not?

5. What did Joseph think of Sheena's card?

6. Did you think Joseph's description of his feelings on Valentine's Day morning was good? Why? **PQE**

7. Why does he compare the name 'Valentine' to disappointment?

8. Why is Miss Glennon a 'good teacher' in Joseph's opinion? **PQE**

9. What do you think of the description of Sheena? Do you think it is funny or unfair?

10. What was your favourite piece of description in this extract? **PQE**

Write your own memoir, describing the happiest, saddest, funniest or most embarrassing moment from your days in primary school.

OR

Write Sheena's memory of the same incident. Don't forget to brainstorm.

OR

Design your own Valentine's Day card, and write a suitable verse for inside.

OR

Look up the following words in your dictionary: tempestuous, ideologically, perpetually, ebbed.

Valentine's Day is approaching. You have designed a special chocolate product. In groups prepare to go before the Dragon's Den looking for investment for this product. You need to think of:

- A name for the chocolates
- Romantic packaging
- A slogan
- A poster

Present your product in groups to the class. **R**

Amazing Adjectives

An **Adjective** is a word that describes a noun.

Read this sentence:
The boy ran away from home.

Now read this sentence with adjectives:
The confused little boy ran away from his lonely, frightening home.

DIVE IN!

Make the sentences below more descriptive by adding some **adjectives.** Remember to put a **comma** between two adjectives but not between the last adjective and the noun.

1. Dave ate his dinner.
2. Aran bought a house.
3. She lifted the saucepan and put it on the table.
4. The goalie lifted the ball out of the net.
5. The rain pounded against the window.

WHY DON'T YOU...

Use the following chant to play a game. Start a rap, beginning with the chant, 'the shopkeeper's dog is an *awful* dog …' and then clap four times … clap, clap, clap, clap. The next person must come up with an adjective beginning with 'b' to describe the dog, the next person 'c' and so on. If you can't think of an **adjective**, you are out of the game!

TAKE THE PLUNGE!

Put ten of these **adjectives** into sentences.

ugly, suspicious, blue, vain, shy, large, bitter, quiet, unhappy, tall, transparent, glittering, wobbly, messy, timid, red, noisy, loud, hideous, stunning, delicious, warm, frozen

A Plate of Peas

Rick Beyer

My grandfather died when I was a small boy, and my grandmother started staying with us for about six months every year. She lived in a room that doubled as my father's office, which we referred to as 'the back room'. She carried with her a powerful aroma. I don't know what kind of perfume she used, but it was the double-barrel, ninety-proof, knock-down, render-the-victim-unconscious, moose-killing variety. She kept it in a huge atomizer and applied it frequently and liberally. It was almost impossible to go into her room and remain breathing for any length of time. When she would leave our house to go spend six months with my Aunt Lillian, my mother and sisters would throw open all the windows, strip the bed and take out the curtains and rugs. Then they would spend several days washing and airing things out, trying frantically to make the pungent odour go away.

This, then, was my grandmother at the time of the infamous pea incident.

It took place at the Biltmore Hotel, which, to my eight-year-old mind, was just about the fanciest place to eat in all of Providence. My grandmother, my mother, and I were having lunch after a morning spent shopping. I grandly ordered a Salisbury steak, confident in the knowledge that beneath that fancy name was a good old hamburger with gravy. When brought to the table, it was accompanied by a plate of peas.

I do not like peas now. I did not like peas then. I have always hated peas. It is a complete mystery to me why anyone would voluntarily eat peas. I did not eat them at home. I did not eat them at restaurants. And I certainly was not about to eat them now.

atomizer – a bottle with a spray on top

pungent – sharp, strong smell

thwarted – stopped, prevented

'Eat your peas,' my grandmother said.

'Mother,' said my mother in her warning voice. 'He doesn't like peas. Leave him alone.'

My grandmother did not reply, but there was a glint in her eye and a grim set to her jaw that signalled she was not going to be thwarted. She leaned in my direction, looked me in the eye, and uttered the fateful words that changed my life.

'I'll pay you five dollars if you eat those peas.'

I had absolutely no idea of the impending doom that was heading my way like a giant wrecking ball. I only knew that five dollars was an enormous, nearly unimaginable amount of money, and as awful as peas were, only one plate of them stood between me and the possession of that five dollars. I began to force the wretched things down my throat.

My mother was livid. My grandmother had that self-satisfied look of someone who has thrown down an unbeatable trump card. 'I can do what I want, Ellen, and you can't stop me.' My mother glared at her mother. She glared at me. No one can glare like my mother. If there were a glaring Olympics, she would undoubtedly win the gold medal.

I, of course, kept shoving peas down my throat. The glares made me nervous, and every single pea made me want to throw up, but the magical image of that five dollars floated before me, and I finally gagged down every last one of them. My grandmother handed me the five dollars with a flourish. My mother continued to glare in silence. And the episode ended. Or so I thought.

My grandmother left for Aunt Lillian's a few weeks later. That night, at dinner, my mother served two of my all-time favourite foods, meatloaf and mashed potatoes. Along with them came a big steaming bowl of peas. She offered me some peas, and I, in the very last moments of my innocent youth, declined. My mother fixed me with a cold eye as she heaped a huge pile of peas onto my plate. Then came the words that were to haunt me for years.

'You ate them for money,' she said. 'You can eat them for love.'

Oh, despair! Oh, devastation! Now, too late, came the dawning realisation that I had unwittingly damned myself to a hell from which there was no escape.

'You ate them for money. You can eat them for love.'

What possible argument could I muster against that? There was none. Did I eat the peas? You bet I did. I ate them that day and every other time they were served thereafter. The five dollars were quickly spent. My grandmother passed away a few years later. But the legacy of the peas lived on, as it lives on to this day. If I so much as curl my lip when they are served (because, after all, I still hate the horrid little things), my mother repeats the dreaded words one more time:

'You ate them for money,' she says. 'You can eat them for love.'

livid —
very, very angry

legacy —
inheritance,
memory

1. Why did the family need to air the house every time the grandmother left?

2. What does the little boy think of the Biltmore Hotel?

3. What is a Salisbury steak?

4. How do we know the grandmother was determined to make the little boy eat the peas?

5. What convinces him to eat the peas?

Write down any memories you have about your grandparents, or any older family members.

OR

Make a list of your favourite and least favourite foods, with one word describing what they taste like.

OR

Describe an argument that you have had about food.

6. How does the mother get her revenge on her greedy son?

7. Do you think this boy was spoilt? Give reasons for your answer. **PQE**

8. Did you like the description of the grandmother's perfume? Explain your answer. **PQE**

9. What kind of person do you think the grandmother was? **PQE**

10. What did you like or not like about this story?

You are a doctor who has been asked to come to the school to educate the students about healthy eating. Prepare the speech you would make. Remember, your audience will take some convincing!

Past Tense

Been there, done that ...

The story *A Plate of Peas* is written in the past tense. This means that it is telling us about events from the past.

Look at this sentence:

She lived in the room upstairs.

Now, if this story had been written in the present tense, that sentence would say:

She lives in the room upstairs.

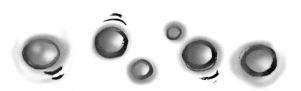

Put the sentences below into the **past tense.**

1. Julie eats an apple.

2. Niall of the Nine Hostages comes to Ireland and kidnaps Patrick.

3. Space is hard to find in the suburbs.

4. The sun shines in the window.

5. The car speeds away and the police quickly follow.

6. The flowers bloom in the spring.

7. The burglar gently eases up the catch and slips in the window.

8. The phone rings and rings but no one answers it.

9. The snow falls on the mountains and melts into the valleys.

10. Trish and Brendan love gardening and plant lots of flowers.

You have just been using what is called the 'past simple' tense. This means that you are describing something that happened in the past, but there is no indication that it will happen again in the future.

Been there, done that, *might do it again …*

Sometimes we want to write in the past tense while also letting the reader know that what happened *might* happen again in the future.

Look at this sentence again.
She lived in the room upstairs.
This is the past simple tense because she lived there once, but there is no indication that she will live there again.

Now if that sentence is written like this:
She has lived in the room upstairs.
it suggests that she may live in the room upstairs again at some point in the future even though she is not living there right now.

This tense is called the present perfect simple tense! Don't worry about the name, but try to remember what it does.

Draw three columns in your copybook and try changing the list of verbs below from the **present tense** into the **past simple** and then the **present perfect simple.** Just look at the example if you are confused.

Present	Past Simple	Present Perfect Simple
I jump	I jumped	I have jumped
I sleep	I slept	I have slept
I do		
I eat		
I smell		
I crawl		
I lie		
I love		
I climb		
I am		
I say		
I see		
I fly		
I fear		
I think		
I drink		
I smile		

Rewrite the incorrect sentences using the correct **tenses.** The words in bold are incorrect.

1. I went to the doctor last week. I **gone** to the doctor but my throat is still sore.

2. I **winned** a race when I was five. I have won lots of races since I was five and I aim to win more.

3. I was in Paris last weekend. I **been** in Paris for my holidays many times.

4. The school bell **rung** late this morning. The school bell has rung late every morning this week, I hope they fix it.

5. I slept well last night. I **sleeped** in many of my friends' houses.

Choose five other verbs from the columns on the left and write three sentences for each: one with the verb in the **present tense**, then one in the **past simple** and finally one in the **present perfect simple**.

Correct little Fergal's homework. Rewrite it for him in your copybook using the **past simple** and the **present perfect simple.**

I done all my homework last night but then the dog eated it. I seen him do it but it was too late as he gobble it very fast. I runned to my Mam and tells her what happens. She said that she rung the school in the past with this excuse and to go and do my homework again. I been doing this homework for three hours now and I already done it before.

43

Round Ireland with a Fridge

Tony Hawks

For a bet, Tony Hawks, an Englishman, hitch-hiked around Ireland with a fridge. Along the way he had many adventures. In Strandhill, Co. Sligo, someone named 'Bingo' suggested that he should take the fridge surfing. Here's what happened …

An anecdote is a short account of an interesting incident or event in a person's life.

The conditions were by no means ideal for surfing, the sea being altogether too calm, but this probably favoured the fridge which was new to all this and hadn't been designed with this kind of activity in mind.

'What's the plan then?' I said to Bingo as we began wading out to sea.

'I think what we'll do is balance the fridge on the board, and then I'll try and jump on with it and ride in on a wave.'

To think the previous evening I had taken him to be responsible.

'Good idea,' I lied, and held the board steady as he lifted the fridge on to it.

It looked surprisingly stable on the board, a fridge's centre of gravity being one of its strong points. However its ability to adjust it in the face of a wave is not, and unfortunately the first wave to come its way was quite large in stature. Despite his prowess in the realm of surfboarding, Bingo had no experience in the art of keeping a fridge balanced on one, and as the wave suddenly forced the board upwards, he lost his grip on the fridge and it slid sideways into the sea. Fortunately, it just remained afloat long enough for Bingo and I to dive towards it and reinstate its position above the salt water. That had been a close one. If it fell in again and we failed to get to it quickly enough, it might fill with water and sink, and the weight of the water within it would make it difficult or even impossible to raise without professional underwater lifting equipment. Foolishly, I hadn't packed any professional underwater lifting equipment.

If I was to lose the fridge in such a way as this, it would make for a difficult explanation as a reason for failure to win my bet: 'Well, it all went very smoothly indeed until I

reached Strandhill and I had a touch of bad fortune when the fridge sank just off the coast, and we were unable to raise it.'

If the fridge did sink, it would also be a considerable inconvenience to bathers who would have to learn the exact position of the wrecked fridge or risk the agony of their toes ramming into its rusting metal shell. In the future, it might even appear on naval charts of these waters, novitiate navigators baffled by the small white cuboid marked as a hazard just off the shore.

We lifted the fridge back on to the board and Bingo pushed the two of them further out to sea, this time paying more attention to oncoming waves. I watched him as he waded out a good distance, my camera poised ready to capture this lunacy on film. He turned and waited, watching each wave in anticipation of his moment. Suddenly a bigger wave appeared and Bingo leapt on his board to join the fridge. The most extraordinary sight followed. A man and a fridge riding the waves in perfect harmony. For a few glorious yards the two of them coasted in with such ease that Bingo looked to have time to open the fridge door and take out a refreshing drink. The onlookers on the promenade broke into a spontaneous round of applause, and from the water's edge Antoinette cheered gamely. It had been done, the fridge had surfed, and what is more I had photographic evidence, provided I didn't screw up with the film again. Okay, the surfers hadn't exactly covered a huge distance, and it hadn't been long before Bingo had needed to leap off the board quickly and save the fridge from another drenching, but nonetheless for a matter of seconds it had been a magnificent victory for Man and Domestic Appliance over the turbulent and untamed sea.

'Congratulations, Bingo. I think that's a first,' I said.

'Thanks. The trick now is to get the thing coming in on its own.'

'Eh?'

'We've got to get the fridge to surf on its own.'

Have we? Why? Honestly, with these people if it wasn't one thing, it was another. Here was me, innocently trying to hitch around Ireland with a fridge, and I kept running into people who wanted to find all kinds of new and exciting things for the fridge to do.

'Oh, all right,' I said cravenly. 'What's the best way to do that then?'

'Well, what I propose is that you wait about here and I'll wade a bit further out, and when I see a wave that looks suitable, I'll give the board a shove and with any luck the fridge will ride in on the board until you catch it.'

What could be simpler?

centre of gravity — balance	*reinstate* — replace	*novitiate navigators* — trainee or beginner navigators
stature — size, height	*inconvenience* — something that causes trouble or difficulty	*turbulent* — wild
prowess — skill		*cravenly* — cowardly

DIVE IN!

1. Does Tony Hawks think that 'fridge surfing' is a good idea?

2. What happens when the fridge hits the first wave?

3. What is Tony afraid will happen if the fridge sinks?

4. Do Bingo and the fridge have any success?

5. What does Bingo want to do next?

TAKE THE PLUNGE!

6. In some ways Tony seems to describe the fridge as if it were a person. Can you find any examples of this?

7. Why do you think Tony gives the words 'Man and Domestic Appliance' capital letters?

8. What is Tony's opinion of the Irish people he's met? **P Q E**

9. Do you think Tony is a sensible person? **P Q E**

10. Pick your favourite sentence and explain why you like it.

WHY DON'T YOU...

Write a story in which one of the following domestic appliances is the hero:

- Hairdryer
- Washing machine
- Oven
- Food processor
- Television
- PlayStation
- Microwave
- Electric toothbrush

OR

Draw a cartoon version of this story using six frames. **R**

THRASH IT OUT!

Divide into pairs. Imagine that one of you is Tony Hawks (plus fridge), and the other is a driver who has picked him up on the road. Act out the conversation that you would have.

Ask the Question and Exclaim!

Question marks and Exclamation marks are sometimes necessary instead of full stops.

We use **question marks** to show that we have asked a question.
How are you?

We use **exclamation marks**:

- To emphasise a point, e.g. Serious crime in Ireland is rising!

- To give a command, e.g. Stop talking this instant!

- To express surprise or humour, e.g. No way!

?!

Everyone in the class must write the name of a person, place or object onto a small piece of paper. These are placed in a pile at the top of the class.

- Write down twenty questions you will ask to find out the identity of the person, place or object that the teacher chooses for you, e.g. Am I a person? Am I a man? etc.

- When you are finished, ask the teacher your questions. Only 'Yes' and 'No' answers will be allowed.

- You may guess the identity of the person, place or object at any time.

- If you guess correctly, the teacher will check your list of written questions. If any questions are missing the **question mark**, you forfeit your victory. You may add questions to your list as necessary, but you may not ask the question unless it is written down.

- The winner is the person who guesses correctly, having asked the least number of questions.

In pairs, write down a telephone conversation allowing one person to use only the words 'Yes', 'No' and *three words* of your choice. The numbers represent the three allowed words. Use **exclamation marks, question marks** and **full stops** to get across how the conversation goes.

Hello? **(1)**

Hello? Is that Laura?

No.

Is that not Walsh's?

No. Byrne's. **(2)**

Is this not 55555?

No.

I must have a wrong number. Very sorry about that!

O.K. **(3)**

Then read out your conversation to the class.

Neither Here Nor There

Bill Bryson

Bill Bryson is an American writing about Europe.

On my first trip to Paris I kept wondering, Why does everyone hate me so much? Fresh off the train, I went to the tourist booth at the Gare du Nord, where a severe young woman in a blue uniform looked at me as if I were infectious. 'What do *you* want?' she said, or at least seemed to say.

'I'd like a room, please,' I replied, instantly meek.

'Fill this out.' She pushed a long form at me. 'Not here. Over there.' She indicated with a flick of her head a counter for filling out forms, then turned to the next person in line and said, 'What do *you* want?' I was amazed – I came from a place where *everyone* was friendly, where even funeral directors told you to have a nice day as you left to bury your grandmother – but I soon learned that everyone in Paris was like that. You would go into a bakery and be greeted by some vast slug-like creature with a look that told you you would never be friends. In halting French you would ask for a small loaf of bread. The woman would give you a long, cold stare and then put a dead beaver on the counter.

'No, no,' you would say, hands aflutter, 'not a dead beaver. A loaf of *bread*.'

The slug-like creature would stare at you in patent disbelief, then turn to the other customers and address them in French at much too high a speed for you to follow, but the drift of which clearly was that this person here, this *American tourist*, had come in and asked for a dead beaver and she had given him a dead beaver and now he was saying that he didn't want a dead beaver at all, he wanted a loaf of bread. The other customers would look at you as if you had just tried to fart in their handbags, and you would have no choice but to slink away and console yourself with the thought that in another four days you would be in Brussels and probably able to eat again …

Gare du Nord – a train station

meek – mild and gentle

patent – obvious

… This is what happens: you arrive at a square to find all the traffic stopped, but the pedestrian light is red and you know that if you venture so much as a foot off the kerb all the cars will surge forward and turn you into a gooey crêpe. So you wait. After a minute, a blind person comes along and crosses the great cobbled plain without hesitating. Then a ninety-year-old lady in a motorised wheelchair trundles past and wobbles across the cobbles to the other side of the square a quarter of a mile away.

venture – attempt

crêpe – pancake

fin-de-siècle – turn of the century

paranoid – thinking that everyone is out to get you

You are uncomfortably aware that all the drivers within 150 yards are sitting with moistened lips watching you expectantly, so you pretend that you don't really want to cross the street at all, that actually you've come over here to look at this interesting fin-de-siècle lamppost. After another minute 150 pre-school children are herded across by their teachers, and then the blind man returns from the other direction with two bags of shopping. Finally, the pedestrian light turns green and you step off the kerb and all the cars come charging at you. And I don't care how paranoid and irrational this sounds, but I know for a fact that the people of Paris want me dead.

1. What is Bill Bryson's first impression of Parisian people?

2. What does he compare the woman in the bread shop to?

3. Do you think he speaks good French?

4. Describe the people who manage to cross the road before him.

5. Why is he afraid to cross the road?

6. Do you think French people really dislike Bill Bryson, or that the drivers really want to kill him? **P Q E**

7. Why is this extract funny? **P Q E**

**WHY DON'T YOU…**

We all like to exaggerate to make our stories more interesting. Try to write an anecdote starting with one of the following sentences.

- *Wait till I tell you what happened to me …*
- *Sorry I'm late, Sir, but I have a really good excuse …*
- *You should have seen the goal I scored in the final …*

- *If I ever have to sit in the car with my family again, I'll …*
- *You won't believe what she's done now. I have the most annoying sister in the world …*

OR

Describe your home town as seen through the eyes of a tourist like Bill Bryson. Do not use real names!

**THRASH IT OUT!**

Bill Bryson tries to buy a pair of shoes in France. Act out the scene that follows. For homework, write out the dialogue.

OR

What do you think the following quote means?

'Sure God help the Irish, if it was raining soup, they'd be out with forks.'   Brendan Behan

Discuss in class whether you think this quote is true or not.

Personal Essay Writing
Paragraph + Paragraph + Paragraph = Essay!

By now, you have probably written lots of paragraphs for homework. Since you are now *brilliant* at writing paragraphs, let's see how you would join them together to make an essay!

Let's say you have to write an essay called

There's No Place Like Home.

- BEGIN with a *Brainstorm* — *Scribble* as many words as you can think of to do with home.

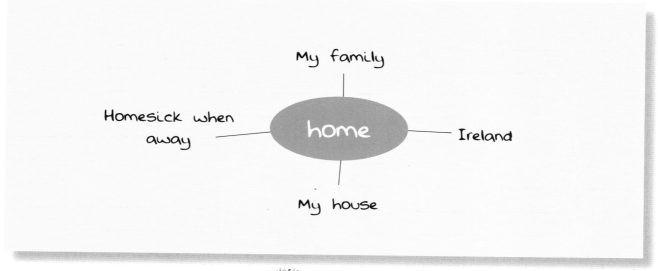

You now need to brainstorm 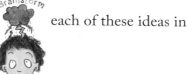 each of these ideas in more detail.

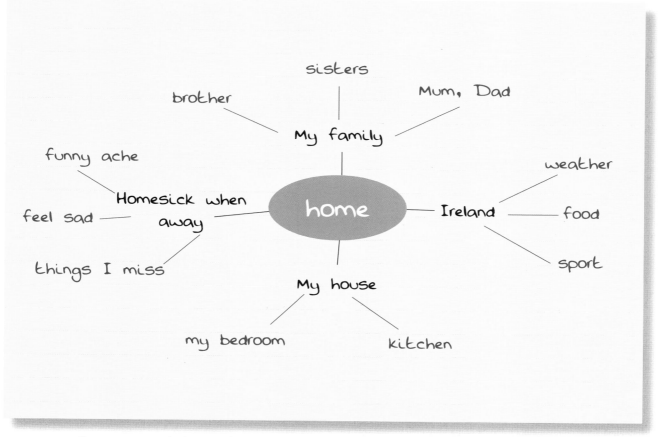

Sometimes it helps to change the colour of your pen at this stage. Now brainstorm around these ideas, focusing on description. Remember, verbs, adverbs and adjectives help!

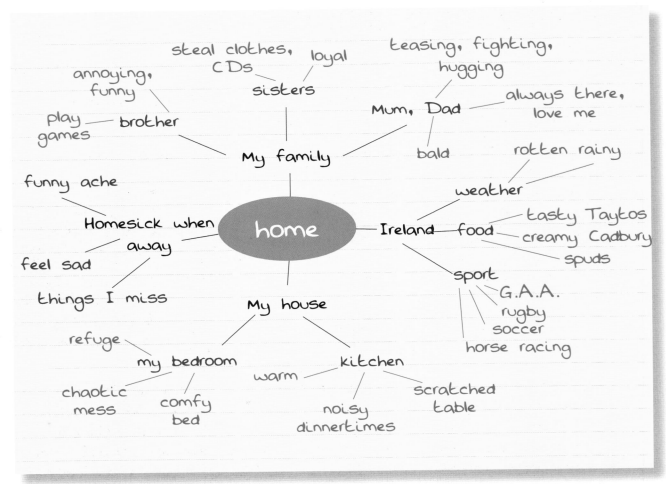

Now write a quick paragraph plan, deciding the order in which you want to present your ideas e.g.

1. **My family** *brothers, sisters, Mum, Dad*

2. **My house** *my bedroom, kitchen*

3. **Ireland** *weather, food, sport*

4. **Homesickness** *funny ache, sadness*

Now you are ready to write the essay. Always try to reread what you've written to check for mistakes and see if you can improve anything.

Brainstorm, paragraph plan and write about one of the following:

- My world.

- Me, myself and I.

- You can choose your friends, but you can't choose your family.

- You'd better watch out, because in ten years' time, I'm going to be …

- Here are a few of my favourite things …

- It was the worst/best day of my life.

A Stink That Smelled Like London

Clare Clark

Tom is a man who worked in the sewers of London in the mid-nineteenth century.
He describes the smells of London on a foggy evening.

Long Arm Tom tipped back his grizzled head and sniffed … At the bottom of the stink was the river. It stretched a good few streets back from the banks, in fact there weren't many places you couldn't catch a whiff of it on a warm day, but in Thames-Street it was as certain as the ground you stood on. You couldn't see so much as the surface of the water through a fog like this one, not even if you hung right over the river wall, but you couldn't miss knowing it was there.

Good writers don't just describe what they see! They use all the senses. Think about this as you read the next couple of extracts.

The next smell you got, when you was done with the river smell, was the sour soot-smudged stink of the fog. London's fog came in all sorts and each one smelled only of itself. This one was a slimy tallow-brown gruel that sank and crawled along the streets, skulking into courts and cellars, looping itself around pillars and lampposts. You tasted it more than smelled it. It greased itself over the lining of your nostrils and choked your chest, distilling in fat droplets in your eyebrows and whiskers. When Tom breathed through his mouth it coated his tongue with the taste of rancid lard, faintly powdered with the black flour of coal dust. It had mouldered over the city for close to a week, rusting iron and smearing soot over all it touched. Through its gloom the buildings looked like grease stains on a tablecloth.

South of the river, of course, the fog got itself mixed up with the smoke. There were parts of Bermondsey where the sky looked like it was held up by nothing but chimneys and the same again in Southwark. Each smoke had its own particular flavour, so as you could always tell where you were. The smoke from the glue manufactories had a nagging acid smell that caught in the back of your skull and made you dizzy, while the soap boilers, their stink had the sickly flavour of boiling fat. The match factories' chimneys excreted a kind of yellow smoke that reeked bad as the alley behind a public house. Then there was the particular drugging smell of hops from the breweries, which didn't smell nothing like reek of leather from the tanneries. South of the river you could smell the change in the neighbourhood when you crossed the street.

Here in Thames-Street the smell was all of its own. In a fog like this one the market was no more than a dirty smudge looming out of its moat of mud, the everlasting clamour of the hucksters muffled even thirty yards off. But the reek of fish, stale and fresh, that

gruel –
a type of soup

rancid –
rotten

mouldered –
rotted

tanneries –
leather factories

hucksters –
people doing
business noisily

53

pungent –
sharp, strong

smelt –
small silvery fish

was stately and self-important as a church. At its base, for foundations, was the seashore smell of seaweed and salt water, and upon these smells were built, layer by layer, reek by reek, the pungent stinks of smelt, of bloater, of sole, herring, whiting, mussel, oyster, sprat, cod, lobster, turbot, crab, brill, haddock, eel, shrimp, skate and a hundred others. The porters that hustled between the boats and the stalls carried then from shore to shop and back again, every inch of them given over to the intoxicating brew of stinks. The stallholders swung their knives in it and sent it splattering across their bloodied wooden boards. Their leather hats and aprons were dark and stiff with the contents of a thousand fish stomachs. Streaks of blood striped the fish-women's arms, their faces, the hems of their quilted petticoats. Fish scales caught in the mud on their boots and glinted like scraps of silver. Melting ice slid from their tables, shiny and thick with fish slime. Beside them wooden crates packed with straw leaked salt and fish fluids into ditches and gullies. Even if you was only in Billinsgate an hour or less the stench caught in the pelt of your greatcoat so that you carried a whisper of it with you the remainder of the day.

1. What is the main sense that this writer focuses on?

2. Pick out what you think are the three most disgusting smells.

3. Would you like to live in this nineteenth-century world?

Pick one of the following and write a sentence to describe its smell.

soap, school changing rooms, a wet dog, newly cut grass, a roast dinner

OR

Invent a name for a new perfume and make a poster with a slogan to sell it.

OR

Mime an action where the class have to guess what it is you are touching, e.g. patting a dog. ℝ

Practise Your Prepositons

Have you ever noticed all the really small words that there are in the English language? Some of these are Prepositions. A preposition joins a noun or a pronoun to the rest of a sentence.

Some important prepositions are: **on, at, up, over, into, through, by.**

Look at the way this sentence changes if you change the preposition:
The cat sat **on** the mat.
The cat sat **by** the mat.
The cat sat **under** the mat.
The cat sat **into** the mat.

Get into pairs. One person puts their pencil case in as many places in relation to their desk as they can think of. The other person has to write the following sentence with as many different prepositions as possible.

The pencil case is … the desk.

See if you can come up with more than ten.

Careful with Conjunctions!

Conjunctions join together two parts of a sentence.

The most common ones are: **and, but, because.**

Look at these sentences:
I like mushy peas **and** chicken.
I like mushy peas **but** not chicken.
I like mushy peas **because** they come with chicken.

Rewrite these sentences using the correct **conjunctions** to join them.

I like Seattle	and	I could buy new runners.
We had a lovely day	even though	chloride.
I saved my money	but	it rains a lot.
Salt is made up of sodium	until	didn't get in trouble.
I left my homework behind	so	Mum lost her wallet

55

Odours Savours Sweet ...

A.S. Byatt

The television screen shows branches and violets. It shows pine forests and sheets of falling white water ending in curls of clean shining spray. It shows meadows full of buttercups and pine forests full of mystery and crisp needles. It is telling you – enticing you – to recreate these atmospheres in your own home with air fresheners, with aerosol sprays of scented furniture polish, with jigging and extravagant canisters of flowery and fruity powder which will 'freshen' your stale carpets, with droplets or waxy cones which drink up the odours of tobacco smoke and shaggy dogs and damp wool and replace them with tangy fruit and flower bouquets. Think how many such smells contend for supremacy in the room with the television. The lavender polish (with its sharp aerosol undertow), the rich peachy freshener hanging in the window, the orris and attar of roses and orange peel in the carpet, the Glade, the Lavender Antiquax, the appley Pledge. Move out into the kitchen, where the floors have been washed with sugary hyacinth disinfectant, where the dishwasher is scented with lemon and honey, where there is a kind of mixed artificial flower scent in the washing machine, and perfumed paper strips making the contents of the dryer smell of essence of concentrated plums and overwhelming extract of cloves, or vanilla, or *pot pourri*, or all at once. You have seen ecstatic dancing women on your screen pressing their noses into heaps of enhanced-white towels, which do not smell of damp cotton but of lightness and freshness, you are told. Does pressing your nose into your own towels induce ecstasy?

enticing – inviting	*extravagant –* over the top	*supremacy –* rule	*ecstatic –* extremely happy

1. What images do you see on the TV screen?

2. What are these images trying to sell you?

3. Pick three of the smells described.

4. Can you hear, feel or taste anything in this passage?

Describe your favourite ad at the moment.

OR

Bring some music without words (instrumental music) into class. Play the music three times.

- The first time you hear the music, write down any **words** that come into your head. They can be anything at all.

- The second time you listen, look at the words you have written and try to think of a **place.**

- After the third time you have heard the music, write a paragraph describing a **place,** a **moment** or a **situation.** Remember to describe it using all your senses!

What I Was

Meg Rosoff

In my impatience, I arrived at the beach an hour early on the first Saturday morning of the January term. The outgoing tide still covered the causeway in a foot of frigid green water, but I was unwilling to hang about in the cold. Removing shoes and socks and rolling up my trousers, I plunged in, finding myself first ankle-deep, then knee-deep, and then, panicking, thigh-deep in icy water and mud, overstuffed satchel balanced on my head, unable (and unwilling) to turn back. I lost all feeling in my feet almost immediately, which rendered me even more clumsy than usual. My arms ached with the weight of the heavy bag.

About halfway across I realised what an idiot I was. The current was so strong that I could easily be swept out to sea and drowned. When I stepped on something that rocked, and slipped sideways, terrifying seconds passed before I regained my balance. By now the food and I were soaked.

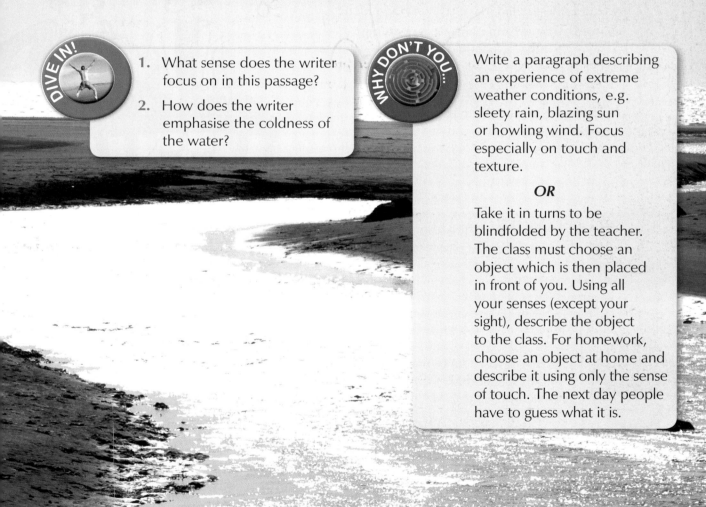

DIVE IN!

1. What sense does the writer focus on in this passage?

2. How does the writer emphasise the coldness of the water?

WHY DON'T YOU...

Write a paragraph describing an experience of extreme weather conditions, e.g. sleety rain, blazing sun or howling wind. Focus especially on touch and texture.

OR

Take it in turns to be blindfolded by the teacher. The class must choose an object which is then placed in front of you. Using all your senses (except your sight), describe the object to the class. For homework, choose an object at home and describe it using only the sense of touch. The next day people have to guess what it is.

Fast Food Nation

Eric Schlosser

Fast Food Nation is a book about the fast food industry in America. In this extract Eric Schlosser visits a laboratory which creates the smells and flavours that are added to food to make it more appealing.

Grainger had brought a dozen small glass bottles from the lab. After he opened each bottle, I dipped a fragrance testing filter into it. The filters were long white strips of paper designed to absorb aroma chemicals without producing off-notes. Before placing the strips of paper before my nose, I closed my eyes. Then I inhaled deeply, and one food after another was conjured from the glass bottles. I smelled fresh cherries, black olives, sauteed onions and shrimp. Grainger's most remarkable creation took me by surprise. After closing my eyes, I suddenly smelled a grilled hamburger. The aroma was uncanny, almost miraculous. It smelled like someone in the room was flipping burgers on a hot grill. But when I opened my eyes, there was just a narrow strip of white paper and a smiling flavourist.

1. Why do you think the author closes his eyes when smelling the strips of paper?

2. What smell really takes the author by surprise?

3. Why does he call the scientist a 'flavourist'?

Pick one of your favourite foods, something that makes your mouth water even to think of it. Your mission is to make everyone else's stomach rumble when they read your description. You must make them imagine they can taste and smell it but also remember colour and texture, e.g. a crunchy green apple or a luscious, tangy, lemon cheesecake.

OR

Write a menu for one of the following places:

school canteen, space station, safari camp, five-star restaurant, Olympic training camp (or anywhere else you choose) ®

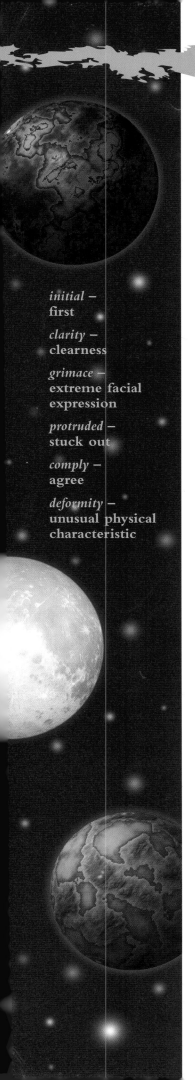

Rocket Science

Jeanne Willis

Adam is fascinated by outer space. On a beach he sees a group of children throwing pebbles at a rock pool. When they run away, he goes to investigate.

It looked like a small, dead boy from where he was standing. Tragic as it was, nothing prepared him for his initial reaction to it, which was huge disappointment. He'd been expecting to find something else and, while he was ashamed to admit it, he felt cheated, even annoyed.

It was only when he turned the damp, twisted body over with the fat boy's stick that he realised why the other kids had freaked out; its face wasn't entirely human. It was such a shock, he thought he was going to puke. He turned his head away and swallowed hard.

Having managed to control the contents of his stomach, he forced himself to look again. Instantly, he was overcome by the Unknown Force that had spoken to him through the *ET* video when he was small. He could feel it sparkling in his veins like an electric charge. For a moment, he was paralysed. Then, the sensation stopped and with blinding clarity, he believed he'd been chosen to witness this vision, this miracle in the rock pool. And it was a miracle, finding an alien on his own patch. Even if it was dead. Here was all the proof he needed to show the cynics and the non-believers that he, Adam Lurie, had been right all along.

He knelt down and gazed at the corpse in awe.

The scalp, he noted, was covered in bluish-black bristles, almost as if it had been shaved. The skull was much smaller than his sister's, and out of proportion to the rest of its body which was roughly the size of a skinny five-year-old.

There was an injury to the left brow, which had puffed up and thrown the face out of symmetry. The slack grimace and the overcrowded, peg-like teeth that protruded from its lipless mouth didn't comply with the human idea of beauty, but perhaps, where it had come from, it might have been considered handsome.

A fat bluebottle buzzed overhead and landed on the carcass. Adam batted it away in disgust, but it was persistent. It turned into a fight, with the bluebottle dodging under his arm and dive-bombing his ear. Finally, he pulled his trainer off, lobbed the fly onto the shingle and smothered it with sand. By now, he felt so protective towards his alien, he felt the slow, horrible death of the fly was justified.

initial –
first

clarity –
clearness

grimace –
extreme facial expression

protruded –
stuck out

comply –
agree

deformity –
unusual physical characteristic

He tried to imagine how his creature might have walked when it was alive. Its spine was curved, which might have been a deformity. There again, this particular species might have humps for sound biological reasons, like camels.

It looked nothing like any of the creatures in *Star Wars*. There were no tentacles, at least none that he could see. There were no extra limbs, no special breathing organs, none of the extraordinary features he would have expected to find on a life-form that had evolved in a radically different atmosphere.

On reflection, he wasn't all that surprised. It simply confirmed what he and Moses had suspected all along; there were habitable planets in other galaxies, similar to Earth. Therefore it wasn't in the least bit odd that this creature bore more than a passing resemblance to himself.

Pulling the neck of his T-shirt over his nose to mask the sweet, sickly smell, he leant over further to study its facial features more closely. The differences were subtle. It was like doing a 'Spot The Difference' puzzle – he knew there were differences in Picture 'A' (the alien's face) compared with Picture 'B' (his own) but he had to really concentrate hard to discover what they were.

Its eyes were closed. There were two of them, positioned on the front of the forehead, but the sockets were much shorter than his and sat in pouches of folded skin. There were no obvious cheekbones.

The nose was peculiar too. It was small with a sunken bridge but the main point of difference was this: there was no groove under it. No nose groove at all. The area below the nostrils was completely smooth.

To look at the rest of the body, which appeared to have two arms and two legs, he would have to remove the filthy rags it was wrapped in. Miracle or not, he was loath to do this with his bare hands in case the corpse was contaminated with deadly spores.

He almost went back to The Black Hole to fetch his goalie gloves when he remembered he had an empty crisp packet in his pocket – he'd been saving it for the book tokens on the back. He pulled it out, ate the last crumbs and decided that although it wasn't ideal, it was the nearest thing he had to a surgical glove.

Pulling his hand inside the greasy bag, he uncurled the creature's fingers one by one and counted them. There were five, but the fourth and fifth fingers were almost half the size of the others. The fingernails on both little fingers were minuscule – no more than dots.

He studied the palms. Compared to his own, there were hardly any lines, just a single, deep crease. It was a Palm Reader's worst nightmare.

His grandmother Marina had read his palm once. She was a mystic and spent her life working the fairgrounds with Grandad Clem. When Adam was small, his mother used to dump him in Grandma's sweaty, red, skull-filled tent in his pushchair. Once, he'd chewed one of her tarot cards. She'd grabbed his hand, told him he had a particularly short life-line and predicted he'd come to a sticky end.

He wondered what fortune she could have foreseen in the floppy little hand he was holding. He shook it gently by the wrist. It was still slightly warm and pliable. No sign of rigor mortis. The poor thing must have died seconds before he arrived.

Adam felt ashamed to be human. Here lay the answer to the greatest mystery in the universe and it had been silenced for ever by a boy with a pebble. Why hadn't he tried to stop him? The kid hadn't been that big. He wasn't even as big as Sonny. He would never forgive himself. More to the point, nor would Moses. If Moses had been there, they could have done something.

He sighed and gave the thin wrist an apologetic squeeze. Suddenly, he felt a soft pulse beneath his fingers, which made him fling the hand away with a shriek. The hand sprang back. The alien sat up, flung both arms around him and fell backwards into the rock pool with Adam pinned to his chest. He couldn't move.

They lay and screamed, eyeball to eyeball, until they both ran out of breath.

minuscule – tiny	*pliable –* easy to move	*rigor mortis –* stiffness in a dead body

1. Why did the other kids freak out?

2. How does Adam know the creature is an alien?

3. What's Adam's first reaction to the alien?

4. How does he know the alien has been injured?

5. How is the alien different from *Star Wars* aliens?

6. What are the main differences between the alien and humans?

7. Why does Adam kill the bluebottle? **P Q E**

8. Why does Adam feel ashamed to be human? **P Q E**

9. How do you think the alien got there?

10. What would you do if you found an alien on a beach?

Draw a picture of the alien based on the details in this extract.

OR

Under the following headings, list in your copybook as many details which Adam noticed as you can:

See   Hear
Smell   Taste
Touch

OR

Write a story about how you woke up one night to find a small but friendly alien sitting at the foot of your bed.

Science fiction movies and books are a complete waste of time!

Have a class discussion on this topic.

Descriptive Essay Writing
Paragraph + Paragraph + Paragraph = Essay!

Remember to:

- Use adjectives, strong verbs, and adverbs.

- Use all your senses – sight, touch, taste, smell and hearing.

- Brainstorm! Look at the example below – your essay title is *A Place I Love*.

1. Begin by writing down all the things (nouns) you can think of:

2. Next change your colour pen and focus on adjectives – remember to think about *all* your senses!

3. Finally, change pens again and add in some verbs and adverbs:

4. Look back at your brainstorm, and do a paragraph plan, e.g.

1. Cliffs
2. Sand and Shells
3. Seaweed
4. Rocks
5. Sea

5. Your first paragraph might begin like this:

As I walked towards my favourite place, a beach near my house, I took a moment to stand at the edge of the tall, powerful cliffs and survey the scene before me. As always, the sight of the jagged rocks, sand dunes and choppy sea filled me with anticipation.

Brainstorm, paragraph plan and write about one of the following:

- My secret place.
- Sleeping outside on a summer's night.
- A crowded airport.
- A huge concert.

- Dreams and nightmares.
- A painting I remember.
- A busy take-away restaurant.
- A seaside resort.
- Inside my wardrobe.
- An afternoon in the attic.

A Tree Grows in Brooklyn

Betty Smith

A character is a person in a story. There are some interesting characters in the next few extracts.

Francie stared at the oldest man. She played her favourite game, figuring out about people. His thin, tangled hair was the same dirty gray as the stubble standing on his sunken cheeks. Dried spittle caked the corners of his mouth. He yawned. He had no teeth. She watched, fascinated and revolted, as he closed his mouth, drew his lips inward until there was no mouth, and made his chin come up to almost meet his nose. She studied his old coat with the padding hanging out of the torn sleeve seam. His legs were sprawled wide in helpless relaxation and one of the buttons was missing from his grease-caked pants opening. She saw that his shoes were battered and broken open at the toes. One shoe was laced with a much-knotted shoe string, and the other with a bit of dirty twine. She saw two thick dirty toes with creased gray toenails. Her thoughts ran …

'He is old. He must be past seventy. He was born about the time Abraham Lincoln was living and getting himself ready to be president. Williamsburg must have been a little country place then and maybe Indians were still living in Flatbush. That was so long ago.' She kept staring at his feet. 'He was a baby once. He must have been sweet and clean and his mother kissed his pink little toes. Maybe when it thundered at night she came to his crib and fixed his blanket better and whispered that he mustn't be afraid, that mother was there. Then she picked him up and put her cheek on his head and said that he was her own sweet baby. He might have been a boy like my brother, running in and out of the house and slamming the door. And while his mother scolded him she was thinking that maybe he'll be president some day. Then he was a young man, strong and happy. When he walked down the street, the girls smiled and turned to watch him. He smiled back and maybe he winked at the prettiest one. I guess he must have married and had children and they thought he was the most wonderful papa in the world the way he worked hard and bought them toys for Christmas. Now his children are getting old too, like him, and they have children and nobody wants the old man any more and they are waiting for him to die. But he don't want to die. He wants to keep on living even though he's so old and there's nothing to be happy about anymore.'

1. How is the old man dressed?

2. What age does Francie guess he must be?

3. What does she imagine happening when the old man was a baby?

4. How does she think girls might have reacted to him when he was a young man?

5. Francie imagines the rest of the man's life. In your own words, describe what she imagines.

6. What did you think of the description of the old man in the first paragraph? **P Q E**

7. What did you learn about Francie's brother in this extract?

8. Francie tries to 'figure out' the old man. What do her thoughts tell you about her? **P Q E**

Draw three pictures of the man described in this extract, capturing the various stages of his life as imagined by Francie.

OR

Look at the pictures of the old people below. Try to 'figure them out' in the same way that Francie 'figured out' the old man in this extract. What kind of life do you imagine they might have lived? **R**

In pairs, interview each other. Focus on likes, dislikes, hobbies, music, sports, films, TV, reading, fashion, etc. Write up each other's 'Personality Profile' for homework. **R**

Billy Elliot

Melvin Burgess

He's an idiot, my brother, I hate him. He's got good taste in music, though. He always listens to it on his headphones when I'm around so's I can't hear it. Like he owns the air or something.

I don't get much time on my own lately except for first thing in the morning before school when me Dad and Tony are out on the picket line. It was better when they were working. I could get back from school and I'd have hours to listen to anything I wanted. Nan likes the music too. Dad thinks it's modern rubbish, but she's too old to care about that sort of thing. She never tells on me. She probably can't remember long enough to know what we were doing anyhow. As soon as Dad and Tony are out the house, I put the music on while I do breakfast. She can't keep her feet still. I can hear her singing along while she's still in bed. Sometimes she gets up and we jiggle round the room together. She does these poses with her arms in the air, trying to balance on one leg and spin around like a ballet dancer – except she's getting on for eighty and can't walk all that well these days, let alone dance.

'Go for it, Nan! Boogie-woogie!'

Picket line – When people on strike protest outside their workplace (Billy's Dad and Tony are on strike.)

Me Dad and Tony try to stop her because they think she's making a fool of herself. Well, but who's to see her? It's just us, we're her family. If she can't make a fool of herself in front of her family, where can she? She should be allowed to dance and listen to music all day long if she wants too, but my brother's too mean to let anyone hear anything except the sound of his own voice.

'I danced myself right out the womb,

I danced myself right out the womb.

Is it strange to dance so soon?

I danced myself right out the womb.'

You know? It fills up the whole house. And, oh, man, it was just … lovely.

I began to dance round the table while I put the eggs in, pretending to play the guitar. That music just makes you move. Me and my best friend, Michael, we used to pretend to be rock stars when we were younger. Michael used to dress up in his sister's satin pyjamas – you know, glam rock – and put on make-up and stuff so he looked like Bowie or Marc Bolan. I didn't care about looking like anyone; I just liked the music. It was great.

'Cosmic Boogie' lasts just long enough to do the eggs soft – the way my nan likes 'em. I took them out, put them in the eggcups, set out the tray all nice and all. Then I picked the lot up, slid the door to her room to one side with me foot, and I went boogieing into her room.

'Whey-hey, Nan, it's the dancing waiter!' I jiggled in there, doing my best to keep the eggs on their feet … and the bloody old thing wasn't there.

I banged down the tray and ran out the door. Me Dad'll kill me if I lose my nan. She disappeared for a whole morning once. The police picked her up in the end wandering around the railway station in Jesmond. How the hell she got there God only knows. Dad thinks she was probably trying to visit someone who'd been dead about fifty years.

I pelted out the back gate and up the road yelling 'Nan! Nan!' at the top of my voice. She frightens the life out of me, Nan. She can't look after herself. You turn your back for a minute and poof! – she's not there. It isn't that she moves all that fast, you wonder how she gets so far. Once she gets going, she just never stops.

I could bloody kill her! I had to get to school. But, well. It's not her fault she's old, is it?

1. How does Billy feel about his brother Tony?

2. Why did Billy think life was better when his brother and dad were working?

3. What tells you that Billy's Nan enjoys music?

4. Who did Billy and Michael pretend to be when they were younger?

5. Why does Billy get a fright at the end of the extract?

6. How do we know that Billy loves music and dancing? **P Q E**

7. Billy's Dad and Tony don't like Nan dancing. What is Billy's opinion?

8. What impression of Tony do you get from this extract? **P Q E**

9. Do you think Billy and his Nan have a good relationship? Why or why not? **P Q E**

10. Would you like to read more of this novel?

Write a letter from Billy to his best friend, Michael, explaining what happened to his Nan. See the personal letter on page 20 for help with your layout.

OR

This novel is based on a film script. In groups of three, prepare a scene showing Tony and Dad's reaction when they come home to discover Nan has disappeared.

Use the following lines to get started:

Dad: Hi Billy, we're home!

Tony: Have you been at my music again?

Billy: I've something to tell you …

When your script is written, perform it for the class. If you are lucky, your teacher might even play the start of the film for you so that you can compare the different versions!

- See if you can find a copy of the song in this extract – it's called 'Cosmic Dancer' by Marc Bolan.

- Play it for the class.

- Decide if, like Billy, this song makes you want to 'boogie-woogie'!

- Bring in the type of music that makes you want to dance and play it for the class.

- Explain why your song is the best!

Awful Apostrophes!

This is the one everyone gets wrong sometimes ... It is the dreaded **apostrophe!**

An **apostrophe** is used for two things:

- When a word or two words are shortened, an apostrophe is put in instead of the missing letters:

  I am   ⟶ I'm   She is   ⟶ She's

  He does not ⟶ He doesn't   They are ⟶ They're

- To show that something or someone **owns** another thing:

  Mary's bag (the bag belonging to Mary)

  The wind's strength (the strength of the wind)

  So if you are ever stuck, ask yourself if you can rephrase it as 'the X belonging to Y'.

If more than one person or thing owns another thing, then the **apostrophe** comes **after** the 's'.

Look at these examples:

John and Michael, two brothers, share a history book. It is the **boys' book.**

Peter has his own book. It is the **boy's book.**

BUT

There is one infamous exception!

The two words **it** and **is**: 'It is a nice day' becomes '**It's** a nice day' when shortened.

BUT if you want to say, 'The dog ate its bone', you **do not use an apostrophe** in the sentence. The dog did not eat 'it is' bone it ate **its** bone. So even though the bone belonged to the dog, it still does not get an apostrophe. Confused? Don't be, *it's* the only exception!

Someone who is really confused about apostrophes has written the next piece. Can you correct it for them? You will have to take some apostrophes out and put others in.

Christmas is one of my favourite time's of the year. Its one of those days where everyone is happy as they get lot's of presents but that isnt why I love it. I dont care about all the gift's, presents or dinners – its the way families come together that I like. Last year my Dads brother came back from Australia with his children. They're the same age as me so we had great fun. I still have my different cousins letters of thanks, as they all sent me cards Mums family are just as nice, they'd drive you mad with all the talk though. Aunty Bridgets voice is really loud. But her three sisters voices are even louder! I really think that Christmas with all its festivities is an enjoyable time.

A Talk in the Dark

Walter Macken

It was a very dark night. The sky was lighted only by the stars. I sat in the nook on the top of the quarry. If I looked over the lip I knew that I would see the water, black and awesome, sixty feet below me, faintly reflecting the stars.

I knew this place well. When I was young, and unafraid, several of us had tied together a few old railway sleepers, and on this frail raft had ventured on the water of the quarry. We could not swim. We knew there was a great depth of water under us and if the raft toppled we would probably die. We thought that added spice to our daring.

I did not feel this way now.

My hand was up to my mouth and I smelled tobacco from my fingers and got a craving for a cigarette. Why I should crave for a cigarette at a time like this, I do not know. I felt in my pockets. I had a packet with me, a crushed packet but I opened it by touch. I held the one cigarette in my hand and threw the packet from me. I heard a slight rustle from it. I could see it in my mind, falling to the water and resting there, slowly becoming sodden.

I had a box of matches. I took one from the box and was about to strike it, when I heard the sounds. I listened. It was a very still night. There was no wind at all, not even a stray one. It was late September. It was not cold. I listened closely.

It was the feet of a person, I could swear. The land around the quarry was rocky, naturally. But there were many tufts of grass among the rocks. I could trace this person coming as if it was broad daylight and I was up there watching. They weren't the sounds that would be made by the feet of a man. They were woman sounds. And not old, but the footsteps of a young one. You can tell these things, particularly now when my feelings were so sensitive.

I pulled well back into my nook below the top. I looked up at the star-lighted sky. This way I saw the figure of the girl. I was looking up, you see. She was looking down. I couldn't see her face, just the shape. I knew the hair was falling around her face, as she looked down. I knew she was slim, and long-legged. Although this could have been a delusion on account of the way I was looking.

If I was deluded about that, there was one thing I was positive of: this girl was going to step off the top into the water of the quarry. I had no doubt about this.

> Much of this story is told using dialogue. Dialogue is a written conversation between two or more people.

I said: 'Don't do it.' Quietly I said this, just quietly, and I knew I was right when she didn't start or scream or show any movement whatsoever. You see, the mind of this girl was gone beyond fright.

I knew she had heard me. She was holding herself tensed. I thought maybe she thinks I am not real, that she just heard a voice in her head.

'I am here below you,' I said. 'You cannot see me. I am looking up at you. Don't do it.'

'Who sent you?' she asked. 'Somebody sent you. Did my parents send you?'

I tried to analyse her voice. I knew I had to be so careful. Her voice was young, but it was dead. She didn't care, you see. She had no interest in this strange happening.

I thought wildly that the chances of this meeting occurring like this would be millions and millions to one.

'No,' I said. 'Nobody sent me. I am just here. I do not know your voice, so how could I know your parents?'

'Somebody sent you,' she said, deadly, sullenly.

'Can you swim?' I asked.

'No,' she said.

'I can,' I said.

She thought over this. 'Oh,' she said then, and sat down on the ground. She didn't really sit down, she seemed to drop there.

'It is dark,' she said then, 'you might not see me down there.'

'I think I would,' I said.

'It will do again,' she said.

'Oh no,' I said. 'Just persuade me.'

'What do you mean?' she asked. There was faint interest in her voice.

'Tell me why,' I said. 'If it is very valid, then I will let you go.'

'You mean this?' she asked.

'I swear, by God!' I said. I said it savagely. I saw her head turning in my direction, but she could not see me.

'My parents are very good people,' she said. 'There are no better parents in the world. I mean they are good. Good is good, you see, really, really good.'

She was silent. She was thinking over that.

'I am their only child,' she went on then. 'I am going to have a baby. I am seventeen.'

'They do not know?' I asked.

'They know,' she said. 'I told them. I have always told my parents everything.'

'And they said?'

'They said nothing,' she said. 'They said nothing. I see their faces. Their faces are full of love you see, but they said nothing. They just sit and they say nothing. There is nothing they can say. My father, he could beat me, but all he does is put his hand on my hair and he cries. My mother says nothing. She is good you see, really, really good.'

'And that is why?' I asked.

'Yes,' she said. 'I do them a good service. I kill me. Their faces will not change. They won't know a deeper sorrow. This is the way.'

'There is someone else,' I said.

'Who?' she asked.

'There is the father of the child,' I said.

She laughed. I didn't like this laugh.

'I don't know him,' she said. 'I am good, you see. I break away from my parents who are really, really good. Some few times. We play away in this game, on Sundays, and we dance after the game and we drink, and I'm not used to drink, and we put out the lights and we kiss, and we wander on the beach, away from the bonfire and the bottles and I don't remember. I don't even know. I just think I have a sick stomach afterwards. You see. Like you take stomach powders to settle a pain.'

'You will kill the child too,' I said.

She was silent.

I struck the match on the box.

'Look at me,' I said. I knew she would. My eyes were blinded by the light. I put the cigarette in my mouth and lighted it. The match went out. 'You have seen me?' I asked.

'I have seen you,' she said.

'Do you know me?' I asked.

'Yes,' she said. I was hoping she would. After all, it was a small town.

'I don't know you,' I said. 'If you know me, you know who I am, and what I am. You know that I am married for about ten years and that we have no children.'

'I think I know this,' she said.

'I want a child,' I said. 'Give me your child. Don't kill it.'

I heard her drawing her breath.

I talked on. 'You and my wife can go away together, anywhere,' I said. 'I am a moneyed man as you know, and when you come back my wife will have the child. Don't kill this child.'

'You are mad,' she said.

'I know,' I said. 'Why do you think I am here?'

'It cannot be,' she said. 'It would be too strange.'

'Truth is very strange,' I said.

'Why?' she asked.

'Because I killed a child,' I said.

'You are trying to confuse me!' She almost shouted this.

'No,' I said. 'Read the papers six months back. Only a small account. A four-year-old child rushes into the road, right in the path of a car. The child died. That was me.'

'Oh no,' she said.

'Yes,' I said. 'The poor father. He carried her in his arms and she had fair curly hair and blue eyes and there was blood coming out of her nostrils. I knew from the way her head dangled that she was dead. Not my fault, they said. That poor father nearly apologised for his child running in front of my car. They nearly gave me a medal for killing this child. And it was my fault. I could have saved that child. I know I could have saved that child. Every minute of every night I see this child. She is my constant companion. I could have saved her. They exonerate me. They blame the child's death on herself. This is an outrage. I killed this child.'

'What about your wife?' she asked.

'Ah,' I said.

'Do you love her?' she asked.

'Yes,' I said. 'But she is good. She is really, really good.'

I heard her sucking in her breath.

The night was silent then. The cigarette was burning my fingers. I flicked it away. It sparked a bit as it described an arc. I could feel we both waited for the sound of it hitting the water. How could we hear a sound like this? We heard nothing.

The girl stood up. She stood up straight.

'Well,' she said, 'you killed a child; you have saved a child.'

I waited.

'You hear this?' she asked.

'Yes,' I said.

'I will carry my own cross,' she said.

'You have taken the weight from mine,' I said.

She didn't say goodbye. She just turned and left.

I heard her crossing the field. All the way, I heard the sound of her heels clearly on the tarmac of the road. I couldn't mistake this.

I took up the small .38 pistol. I had a licence for this. I kept it to protect my money. I never used it. Once or twice for target practice; once aiming it and firing at flying wild geese on the lake.

It made a loud splash as it hit the water. You see, I swim well and that was why I needed it.

I got out of the nook and I stood on the bank. All at once I was as cold as death. All my limbs started to tremble. Now I was deeply afraid that I might fall from the top into the waters of the quarry. I was filled with panic. I got to my knees and hands and I crawled away from there like a sick dog. I was shaking like the leaf of a silver birch, but I got to my feet and I tottered towards the road, and all I could think then was: not who sent me, girl, but who sent you? Just tell me that! Who sent you?

DIVE IN!

1. How do we know where the man is at the start of the story?
2. What disturbs the narrator?
3. What does he think the girl is going to do?
4. What problem is this girl facing?
5. Describe her relationship with her parents.
6. What solution does the man suggest?
7. At what point do we discover why the man is there?
8. How did the man's story make you feel?
9. Did the ending surprise you?
10. What else could have happened?

TAKE THE PLUNGE!

11. What do you think was the most important piece of dialogue in this story? Explain why you think this. **P Q E**
12. What do you think would have happened if the man hadn't spoken?
13. What impression did you get of this girl? Choose three phrases from the story that gave you this impression. **P Q E**
14. What kind of man do you think the narrator was? What made you think this? **P Q E**
15. What sights and sounds were noticeable at the beginning of the story?
16. What overall image remains with you from this story? **P Q E**

WHY DON'T YOU...

Write another story using one of these characters.

OR

Rewrite this story as a script for a radio play. Remember to think about sound effects. **R**

OR

Write a story beginning 'When I was young and unafraid ...'

THRASH IT OUT!

- Put an empty chair at the top of the class. This is now the hot seat!
- When a person sits in the hot seat, they become a character from the story.
- The teacher will select people to sit in the hot seat.
- Divide a page of your copybook into two columns. In one column write the questions you would like to ask the man and, in the other, the questions you would like to ask the girl.
- Take it in turns to ask the person in the hot seat your questions.
- Afterwards, write a brief description of either character based on their answers.

Writing Dialogue *(also called direct speech)*

We use inverted commas or quotation marks ' ' for two reasons:

● When we want to write down directly what someone said:
'Hello,' said Elaine, 'How are you?'

What the person *actually said* goes inside the inverted commas. Notice that the comma and question mark also go *inside* the inverted commas.

● When we are using quotations.
'To be or not to be, that is the question.'
This is something Hamlet says in Shakespeare's famous play.

Try rewriting the following sentences as direct speech. Look at the first example if you need help.

1. The weather forecaster said that it would rain tonight. *'There will be rain tonight,' said the weather forecaster.*

2. Siobhan shouted that she never wanted to see her mother again!

3. The doctor told the little boy not to be frightened because the injection would not hurt a bit.

4. The manager of the shop explained that all the new potatoes were out of stock.

5. Conor begged his father for a new skateboard.

6. Richard welcomed his visitors and told them to make themselves at home.

7. Martha's mother told her to lay the table and then peel the spuds.

8. The lecturer explained that, in the nineteenth century, Venice was a centre of banking.

9. The movie star denied that he had been fired from the picture.

10. Gillian called for her friend Ciara, and asked her to come out to play.

Rewrite the following dialogue inserting inverted commas where necessary:

Sing to me, said William.

Granny's too old to sing, said Granny.

I'll sing to you, then, said William.

William only knew one song. He had forgotten the words and the tune, but he sang it several times anyway.

Shall we do something else now? said Granny.

Tell me a story, said William. Tell me about the wolf.

Red Riding Hood?

No, not *that* wolf, the other wolf.

Peter and the wolf? said Granny.

Mummy's going to have a baby, said William.

I know, said Granny.

William looked suspicious.

How do you know?

Well …she told me. And it shows, doesn't it?

The lady down the road had a baby. It looks like a pig, said William. He counted on his fingers. Three babies looks like three pigs.

Ah, said Granny. Once upon a time there were three little pigs. Their names were –

They didn't have names, said William.

Yes they did. The first pig was called –

Pigs don't have names.

Some do. These pigs had names.

Write out one of the following conversations:

- Returning an item of faulty merchandise to a shop

- Asking your parents to allow you to go to a party

- Reporting an incident to the guards

- Explaining to your parents why your Christmas report is so bad

- Asking someone out for the first time

Remember there are lots of words you can use instead of 'said'. Here are a few examples you could use to make your writing livelier:

whined, muttered, complained, shouted, whimpered, exclaimed, denied, laughed, sighed, whispered, giggled, coughed, roared, screamed, replied, answered, suggested, asked, demanded, queried, wondered, commented

Create Some Memorable Characters!

To bring a character to life you need to describe many different aspects of the person, otherwise your character won't be interesting for the reader.

Mix 'n' match from the following selection, with any other words you can think of, in order to make a few interesting characters of your own.

Take two of your characters and write a story in which they meet.

Environment

messy bedroom hostel airport
quiet churchyard busy shopping centre
college noisy classroom hotel office
TV studio desert island
surgery jungle
neat laboratory stadium

Describing actions

sternly sneakily miserable angrily wickedly
proudly desperately brazenly laconically loudly
silently jauntily dumbly sadly
defiantly moodily

Traits

lazy rude cruel innocent stupid
sweet gullible kind foolish sarcastic
mean cynical brave generous witty
obsessive jealous ignorant
gentle diligent

Type

miser saint student sailor model
teenager clown mother athlete eccentric
nurse bully nerd baby

Features

freckled face twinkly eyes golden hair
wide eyes knobbly knees muscular build
pinched face frizzy hair lanky frame
large feet big smile

77

Write a story using any of the people in these pictures as inspiration for your characters.

Good stories are set in places with interesting atmospheres.

Loser

Jerry Spinelli

Zinkoff has been at home from school for two weeks recovering from an operation.

To Zinkoff there is not one darkness, but many. There is the dark in the cupboard and the dark under the bed and the dark he can never see: the dark inside a drawer. No matter how fast he opens a drawer, trying to catch the dark, the light pours in faster. There is the dark of outside and the dark of inside.

Unlike most children, Zinkoff is not afraid of the dark. Outside darkness does not frighten him. His father has told him that the stars are faraway suns, and the thought of all those suns up there gives Zinkoff a warm and cosy feeling at night. Inside, he seems to carry his own sunshine with him – he's a sunshine bottle – even into the cupboard, where sometimes he hides from Polly without a twinge of fear.

In one respect, however, he is like almost all children: he fears the darkness of the cellar. And even then, it isn't strictly the darkness that he fears. It's what dwells in the darkness: the Furnace Monster.

79

Like most furnace monsters, Zinkoff's stays out of sight behind the furnace when people are around. It's when people leave, when the light goes off and the door at the top of the stairs closes, in that purest darkness – that's when the monster comes out from behind the furnace.

To be in the cellar then, this is the most terrifying thing Zinkoff can imagine. This will be his test.

Perhaps if Zinkoff had not had two weeks to build up a good head of boredom, taking the test would not have occurred to him. But he is bored and it does occur to him and, for Zinkoff, that is that: if it occurs to him, he does it.

One day while his mother is on the phone and Polly is napping, he opens the door in the kitchen and stands at the head of the cellar stairs. He turns on the light. The cellar appears dimly below him, lit only by a bare forty-watt bulb. He counts the number of steps. There are nine. To his eyes they look like nine hundred. Nine hundred steps into a bottomless black hole.

Knees trembling, one sweaty hand on the railing, the other flat against the wall, he lowers himself one step. He's breathing fast, as if he's been running. He sits down.

He sits for a long time. He has thought that after a while he would begin to feel better, but he doesn't. He doesn't want to lower himself one more inch. He wants only one thing in this world, to turn around, take one step back up, turn out the light, re-enter the kitchen, close the door, and go curl up with Polly. He imagines himself doing exactly that …

… and lowers himself down to the next step.

More of the cellar comes into view: the cold, grey, cracked concrete floor; the once whitewashed walls, now grey and streaked with green slime, gashed and oozing sand; the coarse, timeworn planks of his father's workbench. The modern geometry of the oil furnace and water heater seem out of place in this crumbling pit that reminds Zinkoff of ancient ruins.

He lowers himself another step … and thinks he glimpses the furry edge of a flank pulling itself out of sight.

He grips the front edge of the step with both hands. He stares bug-eyed into the shadows.

The Monster speaks.

Zinkoff bolts. Back up the stairs and into the kitchen, into its glorious familiar light, the stitches in his stomach tingling. He knows it wasn't really the Monster. It was really the oil furnace kicking on with a *whoosh*. He knows it, he knows it. Nevertheless he doesn't go near the cellar door.

Until the next day.

DIVE IN!

1. What different types of darkness does Zinkoff describe?

2. Why is he not afraid of the dark?

3. What is scary down in the cellar?

4. Why does Zinkoff decide to go into the cellar at this point in time?

5. Does Zinkoff really believe there is a monster in the cellar?

TAKE THE PLUNGE!

6. What age do you think Zinkoff might be and why? **P Q E**

7. What tells us that he is afraid when he enters the cellar?

8. The cellar is described in detail. What words in particular help to create this setting? **P Q E**

9. How would you describe the atmosphere in this extract?

10. Do you think a bit of Zinkoff enjoys the fear?

WHY DON'T YOU...

Try to remember something that really scared you as a child and write a description of this memory. Try to capture the setting and atmosphere of the event. **R**

OR

Zinkoff goes back to the cellar door the next day. If he gets to the bottom of the stairs what do you think might happen? Write your own ending to this story.

The Princess Bride

William Goldman

Tension occurs when the excitement in a story builds up and we know that something is going to happen.

Inigo Montoya's father was killed by a six-fingered swordsman when Inigo was ten years old. He also scarred Inigo's face. For more than twenty years, Inigo searched for the six-fingered man to avenge his father's death. In that time Inigo became the world's best swordsman, training under the great swordsmaster MacPherson. In this extract Inigo has finally found the six-fingered swordsman, the evil Count Rugen. Unfortunately, as they begin to fight, Count Rugen stabs Inigo. As he prepares to die Inigo begins to hear, first, the voice of his father, and then the voice of his teacher MacPherson in his head.

Inigo was still talking too. It was still 5:42 when he whispered, 'I'm … sorry … Father …' Count Rugen heard the words but nothing really connected until he saw the sword still held in Inigo's hand. 'You're that little Spanish brat I taught a lesson to,' he said, coming closer now, examining the scars. 'It's simply incredible. Have you been chasing me all these years only to fail now? I think that is the worst thing I ever heard of; how marvellous.'

Inigo could say nothing. The blood fauceted from his stomach.

fauceted — poured

Count Rugen drew his sword.

'… sorry, Father … I'm sorry …'

'I DON'T WANT YOUR "SORRY"! MY NAME IS DOMINGO MONTOYA AND I DIED FOR THAT SWORD AND YOU CAN KEEP YOUR "SORRY". IF YOU WERE GOING TO FAIL, WHY DIDN'T YOU DIE YEARS AGO AND LET ME REST IN PEACE?' And then MacPherson was after him too – 'Spaniards! I never should have tried to teach a Spaniard; they're dumb, they forget, what do you do with a wound? How many times did I teach you – *what do you do with a wound?*'

'Cover it …' Inigo said, and he pulled the knife from his body and stuffed his left fist into the bleeding.

Inigo's eyes began to focus again, not well, not perfectly, but enough to see the Count's blade as it approached his heart, and Inigo couldn't do much with his attack, parry it vaguely, push the point of the blade into his left shoulder where it did no unendurable harm.

Count Rugen was a bit surprised that his point had been deflected, but there was nothing wrong with piercing a helpless man's shoulder. There was no hurry when you had him.

Macpherson was screaming again – 'Spaniards! Give me a Polack anytime; at least the Polacks remember to use the wall when they have one; only the Spaniards would forget to use a wall –'

Slowly, inch by inch, Inigo forced his body up the wall, using his legs just for pushing, letting the wall do all the supporting that was necessary.

Count Rugen struck again, but for any number of reasons, most probably because he hadn't expected the other man's movement, he missed the heart and had to be content with driving his blade through the Spaniard's left arm.

Inigo didn't mind. He didn't even feel it. His right arm was where his interest lay, and he squeezed the handle and there was strength in his hand, enough to flick out at the enemy, and Count Rugen hadn't expected that either, so he gave a little involuntary cry and took a step back to reassess the situation.

Power was flowing up from Inigo's heart to his right shoulder and down from his shoulder to his fingers and then into the great six-fingered sword and he pushed off from the wall then, with a whispered, '… hello … my name is … Inigo Montoya; you killed … my father; prepare to die.'

And they crossed swords.

The Count went for the quick kill, the inverse Bonetti.

No chance.

parry – knock away

deflected – knocked away

Polack – insulting name for a Polish person

involuntary – unintentional

Bonetti – sword fighting technique

'Hello … my name is Inigo Montoya; you killed my father … prepare to die …'

Again they crossed, and the Count moved into a Morozzo defense, because the blood was still streaming.

Inigo shoved his fist deeper into himself. 'Hello, my name is Inigo Montoya; you killed my father; prepare to die.'

The Count retreated around the billiard table.

Morozzo defence – sword fighting technique

Inigo slipped in his own blood.

The Count continued to retreat, waiting, waiting.

'Hello, my name is Inigo Montoya; you killed my father; prepare to die.' He dug with his fist and he didn't want to think about what he was touching and pushing and holding into place but for the first time he felt able to try a move, so the six-fingered sword flashed forward –

– and there was a cut down one side of Count Rugen's cheek –

– another flash –

– another cut, parallel, bleeding –

'Hello, my name is Inigo Montoya; you killed my father; prepare to die.'

'Stop saying that!' The Count was beginning to experience a decline of nerve.

Inigo drove for the Count's left shoulder, as the Count had wounded his. Then he went through the Count's left arm, at the same spot the Count had penetrated his. 'Hello.' Stronger now. 'Hello! HELLO. MY NAME IS INIGO MONTOYA. YOU KILLED MY FATHER. PREPARE TO DIE!'

'No –'

'Offer me money –'

'Everything,' the Count said.

'Power too. Promise me that.'

'All I have and more. Please.'

'Offer me anything I ask for.'

'Yes. Yes. Say it.'

'I WANT DOMINGO MONTOYA, YOU PIG,' and the six-fingered sword flashed again.

The Count screamed.

'That was just a little to the left of your heart.' Inigo struck again.

Another scream.

'That was below your heart. Can you guess what I am doing?'

'Cutting my heart out.'

'You took mine when I was ten; I want yours now. We are lovers of justice, you and I – what could be more just than that?'

The Count screamed one final time and then fell dead of fear.

Inigo looked down at him. The Count's frozen face was petrified and ashen and the blood still poured down the parallel cuts. His eyes bulged wide, full of horror and pain. It was glorious. If you like that kind of thing.

Inigo loved it.

It was 5.50 when he staggered from the room, heading he knew not where or for how long, but hoping that whoever had been guiding him lately would not desert him now …

1. Whose voices does Inigo hear in his head?

2. What effect do they have on him?

3. How does Inigo use the wall to help him?

4. What is Rugen's reaction to this?

5. At what point is it clear that Inigo is starting to win?

6. Is Inigo satisfied in the end?

7. What type of person do you think Count Rugen is? How does your perception of him change during the extract? **P Q E**

8. Why does Inigo keep saying, *'Hello, my name is Inigo Montoya; you killed my father; prepare to die'*?

9. What effect does this have on Count Rugen?

10. What did you think of this extract?

Think about where and when a duel like this would have been fought. Pretend you are a film director and describe the set for this scene. What kind of music, lighting and costumes would you use?

OR

Imagine you are doing a sports commentary on the duel. Remember at the beginning it looks like Inigo is going to die and the course of the action changes gradually. Try to capture the excitement in your commentary.

A freeze-frame is like a scene from a film that has been paused. You are going to pretend that you are frozen in a moment in the story. You decide what character each person in your group is playing. Remember to think about posture, gesture, expression and positions.

OR

Try to pick a moment with a lot of tension from this story. Do a *freeze-frame*.

- Practise your moment.

- The teacher will call each group to the top of the classroom in turn.

- On the count of three, you must freeze your moment, and hold it still for thirty seconds.

When the teacher points to you, you must explain who you are and what you are thinking at this moment in time.

Pretend your freeze-frame is a photograph from a newspaper. Write the caption and article that would accompany it.

You are a journalist from a celebrity magazine who has been sent to interview Count Rugen or Inigo. Make out a list of questions to ask the character. Do this in pairs. Take turns to play the journalist, or the character. Remember the person from the story will want to make themselves look good and this will affect the way they answer the questions! Write your profile for homework.

William's Version

Jan Mark

William and Granny were left to entertain each other for an hour while William's mother went to the clinic.

'Sing to me,' said William.

'Granny's too old to sing,' said Granny.

'I'll sing to you, then,' said William.

William only knew one song. He had forgotten the words and the tune, but he sang it several times anyway.

'Shall we do something else now?' said Granny.

'Tell me a story,' said William. 'Tell me about the wolf.'

'Red Riding Hood?'

'No, not *that* wolf, the other wolf.'

'Peter and the wolf?' said Granny.

'Mummy's going to have a baby,' said William.

'I know,' said Granny.

William looked suspicious.

'How do you know?'

'Well … she told me. And it shows, doesn't it?'

'The lady down the road had a baby. It looks like a pig,' said William. He counted on his fingers. 'Three babies looks like three pigs.'

'Ah,' said Granny. 'Once upon a time there were three little pigs. Their names were –'

'They didn't have names,' said William.

'Yes they did. The first pig was called –'

'Pigs don't have names.'

'Some do. These pigs had names.'

'No they didn't.' William slid off Granny's lap and went to open the corner cupboard by the fireplace. Old magazines cascaded out as old magazines do when they have been flung into a cupboard and the door slammed shut. He rooted among them until he found a little book covered with brown paper, climbed into the cupboard, opened the book, closed it and climbed out again. 'They didn't have names,' he said.

'I didn't know you could read,' said Granny, properly impressed.

'C-A-T, wheelbarrow,' said William.

'Is that the book Mummy reads to you?'

'It's my book,' said William.

'But it's the one Mummy reads?'

'If she says please,' said William.

'Well, that's Mummy's story then. My pigs have names.'

'They're the wrong pigs.' William was not open to negotiation. 'I don't want them in this story.'

'Can't we have different pigs this time?'

'No. They won't know what to do.'

'Once upon a time,' said Granny, 'there were three little pigs who lived with their mother.'

'Their mother was dead,' said William.

'Oh, I'm sure she wasn't,' said Granny.

'She was dead. You make bacon out of dead pigs. She got eaten for breakfast and they threw the rind out for the birds.'

'So the three little pigs had to find homes for themselves.'

'No.' William consulted his book. 'They had to build little houses.'

'I'm just coming to that.'

'You said they had to *find* homes. They didn't *find* them.'

'The first little pig walked along for a bit until he met a man with a load of hay.'

'It was a lady.'

'A lady with a load of hay?'

'NO! It was a lady-pig. You said *he*.'

'I thought all the pigs were little boy-pigs,' said Granny.

'It says lady-pig here,' said William. 'It says the lady-pig went for a walk and met a man with a load of hay.'

'So the lady-pig,' said Granny, 'said to the man, "May I have some of that hay to build a house?" And the man said, "Yes." Is that right?'

'Yes,' said William. 'You know that baby?'

'What baby?'

'The one that Mummy's going to have. Will that baby have shoes on when it comes out?'

'I don't think so,' said Granny.

'It will have cold feet,' said William.

'Oh no,' said Granny. 'Mummy will wrap it up in a soft shawl, all snug.'

'I don't *mind* if it has cold feet,' William explained. 'Go on about the lady-pig.'

'So the little lady-pig took the hay and built a little house. Soon the wolf came along and the wolf said –'

'You didn't tell where the wolf lived.'

'I don't know where the wolf lived.'

'15 Tennyson Avenue, next to the bomb-site,' said William.

'I bet it doesn't say that in the book,' said Granny with spirit.

'Yes, it does.'

'Let me see then.'

William folded himself up with his back to Granny, and pushed the book up under his pullover.

'I don't think it says that in the book,' said Granny.

'It's in ever so small words,' said William.

'So the wolf said, "Little pig, little pig, let me come in." And the little pig answered. "No." So the wolf said, "Then I'll huff and I'll puff and I'll blow your house down," and he huffed and he puffed and he blew the house down, and the little pig ran away.'

'He ate the little pig,' said William.

'No, no,' said Granny. 'The little pig ran away.'

'He ate the little pig. He ate her in a sandwich.'

'All right, he ate the little pig in a sandwich. So the second little pig –'

'You didn't tell about the tricycle.'

'What about the tricycle.'

'The wolf got on his tricycle and went to the bread shop to buy some bread. To make the sandwich,' William explained, patiently.

'Oh, well, the wolf got on his tricycle and went to the bread shop to buy some bread. And he went to the grocer's to buy some butter.' This innovation did not go down well.

'He already had some butter in the cupboard,' said William.

'So then the second little pig went for a walk and met a man with a load of wood, and the little pig said to the man, "May I have some of that wood to build a house?" and the man said, "Yes."'

'You didn't say please.'

'"Please may I have some of that wood to build a house?"'

'It was sticks.'

'Sticks *are* wood.'

William took out his book and turned the pages. 'That's right,' he said.

'Why don't you tell the story?' said Granny.

'I can't remember it,' said William.

'You could read it out of your book.'

'I've lost it,' said William, clutching his pullover. 'Look, do you know who this is?' He pulled a green angora scarf from under the sofa.

'No. Who is it?' said Granny, glad of the diversion.

'This is Doctor Snake.' He made the scarf wriggle across the carpet.

'Why is he a doctor?'

'Because he is all furry,' said William. He wrapped the doctor round his neck and sat sucking the loose end. 'Go on about the wolf.'

'So the little pig built a house of sticks and along came the wolf – on his tricycle?'

'He came by bus. He didn't have any money for a ticket so he ate up the conductor.'

'That wasn't very nice of him,' said Granny.

'No,' said William. 'It wasn't very nice.'

'And the wolf said, "Little pig, little pig, let me come in." And the little pig said, "No," and the wolf said, "Then I'll huff and I'll puff and I'll blow your house down." So he huffed and he puffed and he blew the house down. And then what did he do?' Granny asked, cautiously.

William was silent.

'Did he eat the second little pig?'

'Yes.'

'How did he eat this little pig?' said Granny, prepared for more pig sandwiches or possibly pig on toast.

'With his mouth,' said William.

'Now the third little pig went for a walk and met a man with a load of bricks. And the little pig said, "Please may I have some of those bricks to build a house?" and the man said, "Yes." So the little pig took the bricks and built a house.'

'He built it on the bomb-site.'

'Next door to the wolf?' said Granny. 'That was very silly of him.'

'There wasn't anywhere else,' said William. 'All the roads were full up.'

'The wolf didn't have to come by bus or tricycle this time, then, did he?' said Granny, grown cunning.

'Yes.' William took out the book and peered in, secretively. 'He was playing in the cemetery. He had to get another bus.'

'And did he eat the conductor this time?'

'No. A nice man gave him some money, so he bought a ticket.'

'I'm glad to hear it,' said Granny.

'He ate the nice man,' said William.

'So the wolf got off the bus and went up to the little pig's house and he said, "Little pig, little pig, let me come in," and the little pig said, "No." And then the wolf said, "I'll huff and I'll puff and I'll blow your house down," and he huffed and he puffed and he huffed and he puffed but he couldn't blow the house down because it was made of bricks.'

'He couldn't blow it down,' said William, 'because it was stuck to the ground.'

'Well, anyway, the wolf got very cross then, and he climbed on to the roof and shouted down the chimney, "I'm coming to get you!" but the little pig just laughed and put a big saucepan of water on the fire.'

'He put it on the gas stove.'

'He put it on the *fire*,' said Granny, speaking very rapidly, 'and the wolf fell down the chimney and into the pan of water and was boiled and the little pig ate him for supper.'

William threw himself full length on the carpet and screamed.

'He didn't! He didn't! He *didn't!* He didn't eat the wolf.'

Granny picked him up, all stiff and kicking, and sat him on her lap.

'Did I get it wrong again, love? Don't cry. Tell me what really happened.'

William wept, and wiped his nose on Doctor Snake.

'The little pig put the saucepan on the gas stove and the wolf got down the chimney and put the little pig in the saucepan and boiled him. He had him for tea, with chips,' said William.

'Oh,' said Granny, 'I've got it all wrong, haven't I? Can I see the book, then I shall know, next time?'

William took the book from under his pullover. Granny opened it and read, *First Aid for Beginners: A Practical Handbook.*

'I see,' said Granny. 'I don't think I can read this. I left my glasses at home. You tell Gran how it ends.'

William turned to the last page which showed a prostrate man with his leg in a splint: *compound fracture of the femur.*

'Then the wolf washed up and got on his tricycle, and went to see his Granny, and his Granny opened the door and said, "Hello, William."'

'I thought it was the wolf?'

'It was. It was the wolf. His name was William Wolf,' said William.

'What a nice story,' said Granny. 'You tell it much better than I do.'

'I can see up your nose,' said William. 'It's all whiskery.'

DIVE IN!

1. What age do you think William is?

2. Why has William's mother gone to the clinic?

3. What story does William want his Granny to tell him?

4. What methods of transport does William invent for the wolf?

5. Why does William get so upset at his Granny's ending of the story?

TAKE THE PLUNGE!

6. Do you think William is happy about the new baby? **P Q E**

7. Do you think William's Granny is a nice Granny? Explain your answer.

8. Which one of William's 'corrections' do you prefer? Why?

9. How do you know that William and the Granny are trying to catch each other out? **P Q E**

10. Suggest reasons why William wants to be the wolf.

WHY DON'T YOU...

Write William's version of one of the following stories or any other fairy story you can think of:

- *Little Red Riding Hood*
- *Sleeping Beauty*
- *The Three Billy Goats Gruff*
- *Beauty and the Beast*
- *Hansel and Gretel*

OR

Imagine and write the instructions you think might be in William's first aid book for the treatment of a cut finger.

OR

Look up the following words in your dictionary: cascaded, negotiation, cautiously, suspicious, prostrate.

Spellings

Here are some of the most commonly misspelled words:

A
absence
accidentally
accept
acceptance
accommodation
acknowledge
address
appearance
argue
arguing
argument
awful
awkward

B
beautiful
beautifully
beginning
belief
believe
Britain
budget
business

C
career
ceiling
cemetery
character
chief
chiefs
choice
choose
chose
cliff
cliffs
close
cloth
clothes

coolly
college
coming
committed
committee
conscience
conscious

D
deceive
definitely
describe
develop
disappointment

E
eight
embarrassed
emphasise
exaggerate
excellent

F
February
financial
fulfil
fulfilled

G
gauge
glamorous
glamour
government
grammar
grandeur
guard

H
handkerchief
handkerchiefs
height
humorous
humour
hypocrisy

I
immediately
independence
irresistible

K
knowledge
knowledgeable

L
leisure
liaison
loneliness
lonely
loose
lose

M
marriage
medicine
Mediterranean
millennium
mischief
mischievous
monastery

N
necessary
niece

O
occasion
occasionally
occur
occurred
occurrence
organiser

P
panic
panicked
parallel
parliament
permanent
personnel
physical
planning
poem
poet
poetry
possess
possesses
professional
prejudice
privilege
psychological
psychology

Q
quarrel
quarrelling
queue
queuing
quiet

R
really
receipt
received
recognise

	S	**T**	**V**
recommend	scene	tragedy	valuable
refer	sense	twelfth	vicious
referred	sentence		
relief	similar	**U**	**W**
relieved	sincerely	unconscious	weird
repetition	solemn	unnecessary	wool
repetitious	success	until	woollen
restaurant		usual	would
rhyme		usually	
rhythm			

Bleeps and Bloopers!

They're	This is really 'They are', e.g. **They are** going on holidays.
There	This 'there' indicates place, e.g. It is over **there**.
Their	This indicates possession, e.g. Those boys are looking for **their** coats.
Being	This tells you that something is happening now, e.g. I am **being** watched. You normally would put **am** or **are** or **is** in front of the word **being**.
Been	The word 'been' is used for the things that happened in the past, e. g. I **have been** watched. You always need the word **have** or **has** in front of the word **been**.
Its	This 'its' is used for possession, e.g. The ship lost **its** anchor. Here there is no apostrophe. This is an exception to the normal rule for possession.
It's	This 'it's' is really 'it is', e.g. **'It's** the ship that lost the anchor.'
A lot	**A lot** is **TWO** words!
I did it	This shows that you did the action in the past, e.g. I **did it** yesterday.
I ~~done it~~	Here you need to say 'I **have done** my homework in an hour every night this week.' If you want to use **done** you must use **have** or **has** as well.
Scene	This is a **scene** from a play or film, e.g. That film had a great **scene**.
Seen	You must use the word **have** or **has** with the verb **seen**, e.g. 'I **have seen** that film before' and 'She **has seen** that film before.'
Who's	'Who's' means 'who is' in this sentence, e.g. **Who's** at the door?
Whose	This 'whose' means who owns it, e.g. **Whose** coat is this?

Play with Poetry

In this chapter you will learn about **techniques** that poets use including:

- Similes
- Metaphors
- Personification
- Alliteration
- Assonance
- Onomatopoeia

- You will also have the chance to say what you think about the poems you read

- You will try writing some poetry yourself in the Do-It-Yourself poetry section

- And you will have the opportunity to read different poems in the Themed Poetry Section

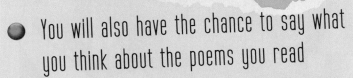

Summer is a beautiful yellow flower which opens at day and closes at night.

King of the Kurzel

Mick Gowar

The Kurzel, Southend:
biggest loudest most
beautiful and brightest
gorgeous pleasure dome a
huge exploding crimson
blur electric blue a
whirling golden gleaming
jewel
sat by a sludge brown sea
All teeming human life left
miles and miles beneath:
the biggest
everything in all the world

The photograph is
black and white
it shows

two people
of about fourteen
in pale grey uniforms
one boy, one girl
The boy at first sight
seems to have a broken arm
around the girl
his hand a

curious limp epaulette
at her shoulder
his hand seems
scared, the intimacy
too much, too soon
they grin:
the girl has
both eyes lightly closed

Kurzel –
an amusement park in
Southend

epaulette –
decoration on the
shoulder of soldiers'
uniforms

the boy is me
the day was
it
the day of days
the outing of
the ATC and GVC

All month I'd prayed:
Oh, let her see me
don't let her see my nose, but
let her see me
I sat behind her
on the coach trip going down
appeared by chance
beside her
on the dipper
My dreams came true
She clutched my hand, clung,
held it harder when
the ride was over
kept on holding …

On the waltzer –
snaked my arm around her
shoulders
She didn't shake it off
When we got off

hers wound itself
around my waist

(I couldn't breathe, believe it
never wanted such joy
to end)

In the throng, that thrill
that thump, thump in my throat
So loud I'm sure she heard
my heart pound Oh, I love you

She kissed me on the coach
– not once, but over and over
and over
And all the spinning, swirling
bucking bronco rides
were nothing, nothing like that
The coloured lights, the crowds
had witnessed
the great moment –
Me, grown-up
She'd shown them all
her lovely arms
around me
like a crown

© Mick Gowar

DIVE IN!

1. How do we know, even in the first verse, that the speaker is very excited?

2. Choose two parts of the poem which show how nervous the boy was.

3. Do you think there is actually anything wrong with his nose?

4. Did he really 'appear by chance' next to the girl?

5. Why does he feel like the King of the Kurzel?

POETIC TECHNIQUE:

The **theme** of a poem is the main topic or issue in the poem. Just ask yourself, what is the poem **really** about?

TAKE THE PLUNGE!

What do you think is the **theme** of this poem?

● Holidays

● First love

● Taking chances

● The beauty of nature

Explain fully why you made this choice, using examples from the poem. **P Q E**

WHY DON'T YOU...

Rewrite this poem from the girl's point of view. Did she fancy him too?

OR

Describe how you think the boy would have felt if the girl had rejected him.

THRASH IT OUT!

In groups, make a list of the worst and best chat-up lines you have heard.

Read the following two poems quietly to yourself. As you are reading, try to picture what the poets are describing, then choose one of the pictures and draw it.

Midsummer, Tobago
Derek Walcott

Broad sun-stoned beaches.

White heat.
A green river.

A bridge,
scorched yellow palms

from the summer-sleeping house
drowsing through August.

Days I have held,
days I have lost,

days that outgrow, like daughters,
my harbouring arms.

Poem
William Carlos Williams

As the cat
climbed over

the top of

the jamcloset
first the right
forefoot

carefully
then the hind
stepped down

into the pit of
the empty
flowerpot

POETIC TECHNIQUE:

A poem is a series of word-pictures. We see them with our mind instead of with our eyes. We call these pictures **images**. The pictures you just drew illustrated **images** from the poems.

I Need Your Love ...

John Curtin

Like cornflakes need milk,
Like fashion needs silk,
I need your love.

Like canvas needs paint,
Like religion needs a saint,
I need your love.

Like silver needs the moon,
Like the sun needs its noon,
I need your love.

Like a ball needs a net,
Like a child needs a pet,
I need your love.

Like a guitar needs a string,
Like a bell needs to ring,
I need your love.

Like an addict needs a fix,
Like a building needs its bricks,
I need your love.

Like a bungee jumper
Needs an empty void,
Like a big wave surfer
Needs a tube to ride,
I need your love.

Like an orphan needs a home,
Like a nomad needs to roam,
I need your love.

Like a medal needs a chain,
Like flowers need rain,
Like a drug needs pain,
Like guilt needs blame,
I need your love.

Like a devil needs hate,
Like heaven needs a gate,
I need your love.

POETIC TECHNIQUE:

A simile is a special kind of image. The poet creates a picture by comparing two things of different natures, using the words 'like', 'as' or 'than'.

When dealing with **similes** the most important thing is to figure out *what is being compared to what*. For example, in this poem the poet used the simile,

'I need your love … like a bungee jumper needs an empty void'.

- The poet's need for love is **being compared** to a bungee jumper's need for height.

- Ask yourself **what quality** of love is being compared to **what quality** of a bungee jump?

- The *thrill* of love is being compared to the *thrill* of a bungee jump.

- Remember 'love' and 'bungee jumping' are two things of completely different natures – this is what makes similes effective!

1. Look at these similes then rewrite the sentences below, filling in the gaps using the words listed.

   longing, addiction, excitement, stability, success

a. 'I need your love … like a big wave surfer needs a tube to ride.'
   The _____ of love is being compared to the _____ of catching a wave.

b. 'I need your love … like a ball needs a net.'
   The _____ of love is being compared to the _____ of putting a ball in the back of the net.

c. 'I need your love … like an addict needs a fix.'
   The _____ for love is being compared to the _____ of an addict for a drug.

d. 'I need your love … like an orphan needs a home.'
   The _____ for love is being compared to the _____ of an orphan for a home.

e. 'I need your love … like a building needs its bricks.'
   The _____ love brings is being compared to the _____ that bricks give a house.

Look at the example below and then try writing your own **similes** to describe some of the following:

Fluffy clouds are like big, soft marshmallows in the sky.

1. Scoring a goal is like …
2. Breaking up is harder than …
3. Eating chips is like …
4. Waiting for the exam results is as …
5. Jumping into the sea was like …
6. My room looks as if … *(you can't say 'a bomb hit it'!)*
7. The lion's roar was louder than …
8. The gas explosion shook the building like … *(you can't say 'an earthquake'!)*
9. A hippopotamus is like …
10. Her pounding head felt as though …

Or anything else you can think of!

POETIC TECHNIQUE:

Did you notice that some similes are very well known? For example 'as tough as leather' or 'as white as snow'. These are called **clichés**, because they have been used so much. Try to avoid using **clichés** in your writing, instead make an effort to come up with new comparisons.

See if you can find any **similes** in your favourite song lyrics. Ask the teacher to play your song in class and, in return, write out a full explanation of the simile.

What Is ... the Sun?

Wes Magee

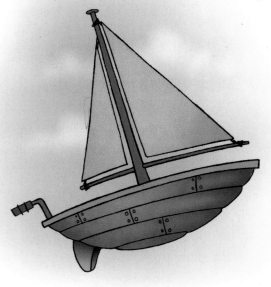

The sun is an orange dinghy
    sailing across a calm sea.

It is a gold coin
    dropped down a drain in heaven.

It is a yellow beach ball
    kicked high into the summer sky.

It is a red thumb-print
    on a sheet of pale blue paper.

It is the gold top from a milk bottle
    floating on a puddle.

POETIC TECHNIQUE:
Sometimes the poet creates an image
by comparing two things of **different
natures, without** using the words
'like', 'as' or 'than'.
This is called a **metaphor**.

Again the most important thing to do is to figure out:
What is being compared to what?

- The sun is being compared to a gold coin.
- The *colour* of the sun is being compared to the *colour* of a gold coin.
- The way the *sun slips* down in the sky is being compared to the way a coin *slips down* a drain.

1. Make a list of three things the sun is compared to in this poem.

2. Using the examples above, explain what comparisons are being made.

Look at the following examples and then try to write your own **metaphors**.

Autumn is golden honey being spread on a slice of freshly baked bread.

Nightmares are frogs jumping all over you.

- Stars are …
- Homework is …
- Duvets are …
- Chocolate is …
- Bare winter trees are …
- Hungry ogres are …
- An empty classroom is …
- Towering skyscrapers are …
- Loud music on the stereo is …
- Losing a friend is …

My Ship

Christy Brown

When I was a lad my bed was the ship
that voyaged me far through the star-dusted night
to lands forever beyond the world's lip
dark burning olive lands of delight
across blood-red oceans under the stars
lorded by the scarlet splendour of Mars.

It is only a bed now spread with eiderdown
and the sheets merciless chains holding me down.

DIVE IN!

1. What does the poet compare his bed to?

2. Where do his voyages take him?

3. How does he make his imaginary lands stand out?

WHY DON'T YOU...

Draw a picture to match this poem.

OR

Write a description of a land you imagine *beyond the world's lip*.

TAKE THE PLUNGE!

4. What new metaphor is introduced in the last two lines? Why do you think the poet does this? **P Q E**

5. If you had to give this poem a new name what would it be and why?

WHY DON'T YOU...

Make a poster using your favorite **metaphor** as the slogan. Look at these three examples for inspiration!

Summer is a beautiful yellow flower which opens at day and closes at night.

Monday is banging your small toe off the door.

Monday
is banging your
small toe off the
door

A tree covered in snow is vanilla ice-cream melting over a choclate log.

a tree covered in snow is ...

..vanilla ice-cream
melting over
a choclate
log.

Indian Children Speak

Juanita Bell

People said, 'Indian children are hard to teach.
   Don't expect them to talk.'
One day stubby little Boy said,
'Last night the moon went all the way with me,
When I went out to walk.'
People said, 'Indian children are very silent.
Their only words are no and yes.'
But, ragged Pansy confided softly,
'My dress is old, but at night the moon is kind;
Then I wear a beautiful moon-coloured dress.'
People said, 'Indian children are dumb.
They seldom make a reply.'
Clearly I hear Delores answer,
'Yes, the sunset is so good, I think God is
   throwing
A bright shawl around the shoulders of the sky.'
People said, 'Indian children have no affection.
They just don't care for anyone.'

Then I feel Ramon's hand and hear him
   whisper,
'A wild animal races in me since my mother
   sleeps
under the ground. Will it always run and run?'
People said, 'Indian children are rude.
They don't seem very bright.'
Then I remember Joe Henry's remark,
'The tree is hanging down her head because
   the sun
is staring at her. White people always stare.
They do not know it is not polite.'
People said, 'Indian children never take you in,
Outside their thoughts you'll always stand.'
I have forgotten the idle words that People said,
But treasure the day when iron doors swung
   wide,
And I slipped into the heart of Indian Land.

DIVE IN!

1. What do the people say about Indian children?

2. What do they really mean when they say those things?

3. Do you think what they say is true?

4. Does the poet agree with the people? Explain your answer.

5. What is your impression of the Indian children?

POETIC TECHNIQUE:
When something that isn't human is given human characteristics, it is called **personification**.

TAKE THE PLUNGE!

6. In this poem the stubby little Boy said, 'the moon went all the way with me, When I went out to walk'. What human characteristics is the moon being given?

7. Pansy gives the moon another human characteristic. What is it?

8. In this poem Joe Henry said, 'The tree is hanging down her head because the sun is staring at her'. Explain the personification of the tree and the sun in this line.

WHY DON'T YOU…

Think of an object and try to imagine what kind of person it would be if it were human. For example:

An iPod would be exciting, temperamental and fun.

A Ferrari would be a show-off with a big attitude.

Choose some of the following objects and write a sentence describing what they woud be like if they were human:

- A comfy armchair
- A sharp knife
- A mobile phone
- A rock
- A French dictionary
- A Nissan Micra
- A gold watch
- A school locker
- A football
- A river

THRASH IT OUT!

The poem is about the 'things people say'. In groups draw up a list of the 'things people say' about some of the following:

- Teenagers
- Old people
- Blondes
- Politicians
- Celebrities

Awash

Cathal Ó Ciardhubháin

Orchestral booms, triumphant tunes,
Bomb-blasted spray sweeps over.
White cotton towers, explode like flowers,
Snow ploughed the waves roll over.
The beaufort beat, soft salted sheets,
Blows breath or flares in tatters,
Rough ragged swells, in haste excel,
Strike strong, fall forceful, scatter.
Above this din, clouds stroll in,
Foretell a twilight dawning.
Dull moonlight skies, storm wasted cries,
As if in joy but mourning.
A sailor stares through tinted layers,
Young witness to nature's warnings.

beaufort − scale used to measure wind

1. Where do you think this poem was written?

2. What do you think is happening?

3. Pick your favourite word or phrase from this poem and say what you like about it.

4. Is this a noisy or a quiet poem? Can you choose words that describe sounds?

5. Pick out examples of **alliteration** from 'Awash'.

People actually use **alliteration** every day. Have you ever heard the line,

Around the rugged rocks the ragged rascal ran?

OR

Peter Piper picked a peck of pickled peppers?

Can you invent some tongue-twisters using alliteration?

Here are some words to get you started:

saucy sisters, bratty brothers, luscious lollipops, tough teachers, fabulous football, miserable Mondays, zany zebras, comfy couches

POETIC TECHNIQUE:
When lots of words in a poem start with the same letter, it is called **alliteration**.

O What is that Sound

W. H. Auden

O what is that sound which so thrills the ear,
Down in the valley drumming, drumming?
Only the scarlet soldiers, dear,
The soldiers coming.

O what is that light that I see flashing so clear,
Over the distance brightly, brightly?
Only the sun on their weapons, dear,
As they step so lightly.

O what are they doing with all that gear,
What are they doing this morning, this
morning?
Only the usual manoeuvres, dear,
Or perhaps a warning.

O why have they left the road down there?
Why are they suddenly wheeling, wheeling?
Perhaps a change in the orders, dear,
Why are you kneeling?

O haven't they stopped for the doctor's care,
Haven't they reined their horses, horses?
Why, they are none of them wounded, dear,
None of these forces.

O is it the parson they want with white hair,
Is it the parson, is it, is it?
No, they are passing his gateway, dear,
Without a visit.

O it must be the farmer who lives so near,
It must be the farmer so cunning, so cunning?
They have passed the farm already, dear,
And now they are running.

O where are you going? Stay with me here!
Were the vows you swore me deceiving,
deceiving?
No, I promised to love you dear,
But I must be leaving.

O it's broken the lock and splintered the door,
O it's the gate where they're turning, turning,
Their feet are heavy on the floor,
And their eyes are burning.

A ballad is a poem that tells a story which is
sometimes put to music.

DIVE IN!

1. What is the first sound in the poem?

2. What is shining brightly?

3. How do you know that one of the speakers is becoming more and more worried?

4. What kind of person is answering the questions?

5. How does the poem end?

TAKE THE PLUNGE!

6. What questions does this poem raise in your mind?

7. Can you find three examples of alliteration in the poem? (The use of a repeated word can count.)

8. How does the repetition of certain words make this poem more exciting?

P Q E

POETIC TECHNIQUE:

This poem has a very strong beat. In poetry this is called **rhythm**.

WHY DON'T YOU...

In pairs work out how many stressed syllables or 'beats' there are in the first line. Do the same thing with the rest of the verse. Report back to the class.

POETIC TECHNIQUE:

A **syllable** is a unit of sound e.g. to-ma-to has three sounds, so it has three syllables. The number of syllables in a line can also give it a **rhythm**.

OR

Split into groups and read this poem out loud. Try to think of ways of emphasising the beat. Maybe you could:

- Read a line each
- Shout certain words or phrases
- Add extra sound effects
- Read some words together and some words alone
- Emphasise words with alliteration or ones that are repeated
- Have music in the background

Don't do this unless the people next door are friendly!

Hugger Mugger

Kit Wright

I'd sooner be
Jumped and thumped and dumped,

I'd sooner be
Slugged and mugged… than *hugged*…

And clobbered with a slobbering
Kiss by my Auntie Jean:

You know what I mean:

Whenever she comes to stay,
You know you're bound

To get one.
A   quick
      short
      peck
      would
      be
      OK.
But this is a
Whacking great
Smacking great
Wet one!

All whoosh and spit
And crunch and squeeze
And '*Dear* little boy!'

And 'Auntie's missed you!'
And 'Come to Auntie, she
Hasn't *kissed* you!'
Please don't do it, Auntie,
PLEASE!
Or if you've absolutely
Got to,

And nothing on *earth* can persuade you
Not to,

The trick
Is to make it
Quick,

You know what I mean?

For as things are,
I really would far,

Far sooner be
Jumped and thumped and dumped,

I'd sooner be
Slugged and mugged… than *hugged*…

And clobbered with a slobbering
Kiss by my Auntie

Jean!

POETIC TECHNIQUE:

When a vowel sound (a,e,i,o,u) is repeated in a line it is called **assonance**. For example, ph*o*ne/h*o*me, br*a*ve/v*a*in. Notice it is the vowel **sound** and not just the vowel letter that creates assonance.

DIVE IN!

1. There is assonance in the title of this poem 'Hugger Mugger'. Can you find three more examples?

POETIC TECHNIQUE:

Words that **rhyme** often have assonance – this makes them sound the same. For example, *the cat sat on the mat.*

2. Look back at the examples you picked for **assonance**. Did any of them rhyme?

3. Can you find other words that rhyme, even if they're not on the same line?

WHY DON'T YOU...

Look at these revised first lines from famous nursery rhymes. See if you can complete an updated version. Try to keep the rhythm close to the original! Look at the example for help..

> Baa, baa black sheep
>
> Have you any ink?
>
> Yes sir, Yes sir,
>
> Your printer's on the blink!

- Little Bo Peep got into the Jeep …
- Humpty Dumpty sat on the bus …
- Jack and Jill met up with Bill …
- Twinkle, Twinkle little ring …
- Mary had a little car …

OR

In pairs, rewrite this poem as dialogue for a scene in a TV soap. Act out Auntie Jean's visit for the class.

THRASH IT OUT!

Do you like R&B or hip-hop music? Usually these have great rhythm and rhyme. Why not bring in a piece of music to the class and discuss the beat!

Long ago people believed that the fairies sometimes stole children and replaced them with fairy children or 'changelings'.

The Stolen Child

W. B. Yeats

Where dips the rocky highland
Of Sleuth Wood in the lake,
There lies a leafy island
Where flapping herons wake
The drowsy water-rats;
There we've hid our faery vats,
Full of berries
And of reddest stolen cherries.
Come away, O human child!
To the waters and the wild
With a faery, hand in hand,
For the world's more full of weeping than you
  can understand.

Where the waves of moonlight glosses
The dim grey sands with light,
Far off by furthest Rosses
We foot it all the night,
Weaving olden dances,
Mingling hands and mingling glances
Till the moon has taken flight;
To and fro we leap
And chase the froth bubbles,
While the world is full of troubles
And is anxious in its sleep.
Come away, O human child!
To the waters and the wild
With a faery, hand in hand,
For the world's more full of weeping than you
  can understand.

Where the wandering water gushes
From the hills above Glen-Car,
In pools among the rushes
That scarce could bathe a star,
We seek for slumbering trout
And whispering in their ears
Give them unquiet dreams;
Leaning softly out
From ferns that drop their tears
Over the young streams.
Come away, O human child!
To the waters and the wild
With a faery, hand in hand,
For the world's more full of weeping than you
  can understand.

Away with us he's going,
The solemn-eyed:
He'll hear no more the lowing
Of the calves on the warm hillside
Or the kettle on the hob
Sing peace into his breast,
Or see the brown mice bob
Round and round the oatmeal-chest.
For he comes, the human child,
To the waters and the wild
With a faery, hand in hand,
From a world more full of weeping than he
  can understand.

1. The first verse describes where the fairies live. What details did you notice?

2. In the chorus, the fairies try to lure the child away with them. Why do they want to take the child?

3. In the second verse, where are the fairies, and what are they doing?

4. The third verse is very quiet. What words tell you this?

5. What happens in the final verse?

6. Do you think the poem is happy or sad?

7. Look carefully at the language in the chorus. What makes it sound so magical? You might look for **alliteration, assonance, and rhyme.** ⓅⓆⒺ

8. What is the atmosphere in the child's home? ⓅⓆⒺ

9. Do you think the child will have a better life with the fairies?

Write a newspaper article describing the disappearance of a child. Remember this is a serious issue, so you must show this in the language you use.

In pairs, write a list of at least ten superstitions that you know.

Noise

Jessie Pope

I like noise.
The whoop of a boy, the thud of a hoof,
The rattle of rain on a galvanized roof,
The hubbub of traffic, the roar of a train,
The throb of machinery numbing the brain,
The switching of wires in an overhead tram,
The rush of the wind, a door on the slam,
The boom of the thunder, the crash of the
  waves,
The din of a river that races and raves,
The crack of a rifle, the clank of a pail,
The strident tattoo of a swift-slapping sail –
From any old sound that the silence destroys
Arises a gamut of soul-stirring joys.
I like noise.

DIVE IN!

1. Choose three words that you like from this poem that describe sounds.

2. Does any line in particular remind you of a sound you like? For example, 'the rattle of rain on a galvanized roof' might remind you of listening to rain on the roof at night.

3. There is a lot of **onomatopoeia** in the poem 'Noise'. Can you find some examples?

POETIC TECHNIQUE:
When a word imitates the sound it is describing it is called **onomatopoeia**. For example, the tick-tock of the clock, the buzzing of the bee.

115

Try finding some **onomatopoeic** words to describe the sounds made by:

- Breaking glass
- Creeping mice
- Cheering crowds
- High winds
- Pouring rain
- Loud music
- Knocking on the door
- End of school bell
- Gossiping girls
- Grand Prix starting grids

Imagine you are operating one of the following machines:

- A PlayStation
- A JCB
- A tractor
- A lawnmower
- A speedboat
- A food processor
- A microwave (or any other machine)

In class, create all the sounds the machine would make. Perform your 'machine symphony' with the rest of the class.

Snow

Softly sweeps
The silent streets.
A whispering whirl,
of wonder.

Write a short poem like 'Snow' with any of the following titles:

- Wind
- Thunder
- Goal
- Whisper
- Crash

Try to use **onomatopoeia** as this poet has done.

The Terrible People

Ogden Nash

People who have what they want are very fond of telling people who haven't what they want that they really don't want it.

And I wish I could afford to gather all such people into a gloomy castle on the Danube and hire half a dozen capable Draculas to haunt it.

I don't mind their having a lot of money, and I don't care how they employ it.

But I do think that they damn well ought to admit they enjoy it.

But no, they insist on being stealthy

About the pleasures of being wealthy,

And the possession of a handsome annuity

Makes them think that to say how hard it is to make both ends meet is their bounden duity.

You cannot conceive of an occasion

Which will find them without some suitable evasion.

Yes indeed, with argument they are very fecund;

Their first point is that money isn't everything, and that they have no money anyhow is their second.

Some people's money is merited,

And other people's is inherited,

But wherever it comes from,

They talk about it as if it were something you got pink gums from.

Perhaps indeed the possession of wealth is constantly distressing,

But I should be quite willing to assume every curse of wealth if I could at the same time assume every blessing.

The only incurable troubles of the rich are the troubles that money can't cure,

Which is a kind of trouble that is even more troublesome if you are poor.

Certainly there are lots of things in life that money won't buy, but it's very funny –

Have you ever tried to buy them without money?

Annuity –
yearly allowance

Fecund –
prolific, producing a
lot of something

DIVE IN!

1. What are people who have what they want fond of doing?

2. What would the poet like to do to such people?

3. What does he want them to admit?

4. People with money make two "suitable evasions". What are they?

5. Did you like the end of the poem?

WHY DON'T YOU...

Write a letter from a rich person responding to Ogden Nash's poem.

OR

Perform part of this poem as if it were a speech and you were delivering it to one of the following audiences:

- Your best friends at a sleepover
- In a room full of rich people
- A group of five year olds
- In a homeless shelter
- An annual political party conference

Choose which part of the poem you want to read, and decide what tone of voice you will read it in. This will depend on how you think your audience will react! You might like to shout in some cases and whisper in others.

POETIC TECHNIQUE:

When you talk to someone you can change the meaning of what you say by changing your tone of voice. For example, you could say 'yes' in a happy tone, or 'yes' in a grumpy tone, letting your listener know how you are feeling. Poems also have a **tone**. This is the tone of voice of the poet or the speaker in the poem.

TAKE THE PLUNGE!

6. If you had to read this poem out loud, what tone of voice would you use and why?

7. What is the poet's attitude to money?

8. Did you think this poem was funny? Why or why not? **P Q E**

A Birthday

Christina Rosetti

My heart is like a singing bird
Whose nest is in a watered shoot:
My heart is like an apple tree
Whose boughs are bent with thickset fruit;
My heart is like a rainbow shell
That paddles on a halcyon sea;
My heart is gladder than all these
Because my love is come to me.

Raise me on a dais of silk and down;
Hang it with vair and purple dyes;
Carve it in doves and pomegranates,
And peacocks with a hundred eyes;
Work it in gold and silver grapes,
In leaves and silver fleurs-de-lys;
Because the birthday of my life
Is come, my love is come to me.

Halcyon —
calm, peaceful and
happy

Dais —
a raised platform for a
throne

Vair —
a type of fur

DIVE IN!

1. Why is the poet happy?
2. How is she decorating the room in the second verse?
3. Which line did you like best in this poem?

POETIC TECHNIQUE:

The main emotion in a poem is called the **mood**. Sometimes this influences the tone.

TAKE THE PLUNGE!

4. This poem has an extremely happy mood. Pick out two lines that you think prove this, and explain your choice. **PQE**

5. Pick your favourite simile from the first verse and explain why you like it. **PQE**

WHY DON'T YOU...

Write a list of things that make you happy.

OR

Imagine that you are a party planner. Write a set of instructions on how to decorate and prepare for a 'Sweet Sixteen' party. Money is no object! Remember to think about the following areas:

- Food
- Music
- Guest list
- Decorating supplies
- Birthday cake
- Presents

THRASH IT OUT!

Have a class discussion based on the following statement:

Money can't buy happiness ...

The Listeners

Walter de la Mare

'Is there anybody there?' said the Traveller,
          Knocking on the moonlit door;
And his horse in the silence champed the grasses
          Of the forest's ferny floor:
And a bird flew up out of the turret,
          Above the Traveller's head:
And he smote on the door again a second time;
          'Is there anybody there?' he said.
But no one descended to the Traveller;
          No head from the leaf-fringed sill
Leaned over and looked into his grey eyes,
          Where he stood perplexed and still.
But only a host of phantom listeners
          That dwelt in the lone house then
Stood listening in the quiet of the moonlight
          To that voice from the world of men:
Stood thronging the faint moonbeams on the dark stair,
          That goes down to the empty hall,
Hearkening in an air stirred and shaken
          By the lonely Traveller's call.
And he felt in his heart their strangeness,
          Their stillness answering his cry,
While his horse moved, cropping the dark turf,
          'Neath the starred and leafy sky;
For he suddenly smote on the door, even
          Louder, and lifted his head: –
'Tell them I came, and no one answered,
          That I kept my word,' he said.
Never the least stir made the listeners,
          Though every word he spake
Fell echoing through the shadowiness of the still house
          From the one man left awake:
Ay, they heard his foot upon the stirrup,
          And the sound of iron on stone,
And how the silence surged softly backward,
          When the plunging hoofs were gone.

turret —	smote —	thronging —	hearkening —
very top of	hit	crowding	listening
the roof			

1. Why do you think the Traveller came to this house?

2. Reread the first six lines. What kind of place do you picture?

3. Is there anyone in the house?

4. Why do you think the Traveller says, 'Tell them I came, and no-one answered' if no-one is listening?

5. How do you feel by the end of the poem?

6. The Traveller asks the same question twice in this poem. Choose two words from the options below that describe the **tone** of these questions. Explain your choices. **P Q E**

   jolly, anxious, angry, cold, puzzled, snobby, insistent, lazy

7. He makes a statement near the end of the poem, and uses a different tone. Choose a word to describe this **tone**. **P Q E**

   defiant, weak, frightened, determined

8. What words would you use to describe the **atmosphere** in this poem? **P Q E**

9. Which part of the poem did you think was atmospheric and why?

10. Can you describe a place with a similar **atmosphere** to the place in this poem?

Write down any questions you would like to ask the Traveller or the listeners in this poem.

OR

Look for a photograph in a magazine, or draw a picture, that you think could be used to illustrate this poem.

OR

Try to find a piece of music that captures the **atmosphere** of 'The Listeners'. Explain your choice.

POETIC TECHNIQUE:

The **atmosphere** of a poem is linked to the setting of the poem; it depends on where the poem is taking place. This influences our feelings.

DON'T FORGET THAT:

The **theme** of a poem is the main topic or issue involved. Just ask yourself, what is the poem really about? For example, 'King of the Kurzel', is about first love.

A poem is a series of word-pictures. We see them with our mind instead of with our eyes. We call these pictures **images**.

A **simile** is a special kind of image. The poet creates a picture by comparing two things of *different natures,* using the words 'like', 'as' or 'than'. In 'Hawkmoon 269' Bono wrote, 'I need your love … like a desert needs rain.'

Sometimes the poet creates an image by comparing two things of *different natures* **without** using the words 'like', 'as', or 'than'. This is called a **metaphor.** In 'What Is … the Sun?' Wes Magee called the sun, 'an orange dinghy sailing across a calm sea'.

When an inanimate object is given human characteristics, it is called **personification.** In 'Indian Children Speak' the moon is described as being 'kind'.

When lots of words in a poem start with the same letter, it is called **alliteration**. For example in the poem 'Awash' the waves are described as 'soft salted sheets' of water. Alliteration gives a line a beat. In poetry this is called **rhythm**.

DON'T FORGET THAT:

When a vowel sound (a,e,i,o,u) is repeated in a line, it is called **assonance.** For example 'ph<u>o</u>ne/h<u>o</u>me', 'br<u>a</u>ve/v<u>ai</u>n'. Notice that it is the vowel **sound** and not just the vowel letter that creates assonance. Words that **rhyme** often have assonance; this makes them sound the same. In 'Hugger Mugger' for example, the speaker says he'd rather be 'Jumped and thumped and dumped'.

When a word imitates the sound it is describing, it is called **onomatopoeia.** Examples include the **tick-tock** of the clock, the **buzzing** of the bee. In the poem 'Noise' Jessie Pope describes the **thud** of a hoof.

When you talk to someone, you can change the meaning of what you say by changing your tone of voice. For example, you could say 'yes' in a happy tone, or 'yes' in a grumpy tone, letting your listener know how you are feeling. Poems also have a **tone.** This is the **tone** of voice of the poet or the speaker in the poem. In 'The Terrible People' the tone of the poem is one of annoyance.

The main emotion in a poem is called the **mood.** Sometimes this influences the tone. The mood of 'A Birthday' is very happy.

The **atmosphere** of a poem is linked to the setting of the poem. Where the poem is taking place can influence our feelings. For example, 'The Listeners' takes place in a moonlit forest, which creates a spooky atmosphere.

Do-It-Yourself Poetry

Shaping Poems

Poems come in lots of different shapes and sizes. They can rhyme or not. The one thing they all have in common is that the words have been carefully chosen, for the images they suggest and the sounds they create.

Acrostics

Roger McGough

A favourite literary devi

Ce is the one whe

Re the first letter

Of each line spell

S out the subject the poe

T wishes to write about.

I must admit, I

Can't see the point myself.

Blackboard
Like a distant galaxy
Aliens take the
Chalk and from their planet
Kronos, sprinkle the
Black moonless night
Over with white stars
After the invasion
Reading is
Demolished.

Blackboard hangs there
Looming,
Awful
Chalk carrying monster!
Kneel
Before it bored students
Or scribble frantic notes
And
Recite
Dead poems.

Write an acrostic poem on one of these words:

ELEPHANT   MORNING   CROCODILE   WINTER   SCHOOL   WAVE

TRAFFIC   SEAGULL   TRACTOR   SKYSCRAPER   ICE-CREAM   FOOTBALL

Limericks
Limerick

John Irwin

A limerick's cleverly versed-
The second line rhymes with the first;
The third one is short,
The fourth's the same sort,
And the last line is often the worst.

There Was an Old Man

Edward Lear

There was an Old Man with a beard,
Who said, 'It is just as I feared!-
Two Owls and a Hen,
four Larks and a Wren,
Have all built their
nests in my beard!'

WHY DON'T YOU...

Use these opening lines to write your own limericks:

- A curly haired man from Ardee …
- A silly old sod from abroad …

- I have a big sister called Sally …
- There once was a girl from our town …
- A sailor who came from Tahiti …
- While trapped on the jam-packed M50 …

Kennings

These were poems the Vikings liked! Take a topic and then try and come up with as many two-word descriptions of it as possible.

TV
Goggle-box
Politician-mocks
Reality-rocks
Picture-maker
Imagination-shaker
Hypnotic-faker
Time-taker
Drama-displayer
Boredom-slayer
Laughter-inducer
Tears-producer

WHY DON'T YOU...

Write a kenning (or two) based on some of these topics.

iPods, seaside, coffee, squirrels, soccer, Xbox, storms, homework, chips, swimming, cats, or anything else you can think of!

Haiku

Haiku is a type of poetry that originally came from Japan.

- Each poem has only three lines
- The entire poem only has 17 syllables
- There are five syllables in the first line
- There are seven in the second line
- There are five in the third line

The aim of the poem is to capture a fleeting moment of beauty. As you will see not *all* poets stick to *all* these rules!

> **POETIC TECHNIQUE:**
> A **syllable** is a unit of sound. We count the number of sounds in the words and that tells us the number of syllables.
> For example:
> toy = one sound = one syllable
> brother = two sounds = two syllables
> personification = six sounds = six syllables

Haiku

Roger McGough

Snowman in a field
listening to the raindrops
wishing him farewell.

Haiku

John Cooper Clarke

To convey one's mood
in seventeen syllables
is very diffic

Uphill

David Harmer

My battered bike groans
Two wandering wheels wobble
Twisted spokes shout 'No!'

Sometimes poets put haiku on the same topic together to make one long poem.

Four Seasons Haiku

Adrian Henri

1
yellow rapefields glow;
hedges dipped in mayblossom:
cream in a green bowl.

2
flags hang limp from masts;
buddleias flop exhausted
on August pavements.

3
folding up fruit-nets;
already a trawl of leaves
in their green meshes.

4
take away one word:
a tall chimney collapses
in the winter wood.

Divide into groups. Choose a topic from the list below. Assign one of the topics to each group. Assign each person a word and write a haiku on that word. Put the four haiku together to make a long poem. Decide on an illustration for the poem and create a 'haiku corner' in the classroom to display the results.

CITY: traffic, buildings, shops, people

NATURE: sea, forest, mountain, sky

SCHOOL: classroom, teacher, students, homework

FAMILY: mother, father, brothers, sisters

HOSPITAL: doctors, nurses, surgery, patients

TRAVEL: suitcases, airport, sun, tourists

FOOD: sweet, savoury, favourites, yuck!

SPORT: winning, losing, watching, hating

Autobiographical Poetry

The best inspiration for your poetry is you!

1. Draw a line down the centre of your page.

2. Put a heading on each column: 'Things that are important to me' and 'Things not so important to me'.

3. Write a list of these things in the two columns. Like the example below:

Things that are important to me ...
My mammy's brown bread
Home and Away
Manchester United

Things not so important to me ...
Homework
Mortgages
Insects

4. Now you are going to write a poem called **CREDO**. This is a list of beliefs.

5. Start each line with the words 'I believe ...' or 'I do not believe ...'

CREDO
I believe in my mammy's brown bread.
I do not believe in mortgages.
I believe in Home and Away.
I do not believe in homework.
I believe in Manchester United.
I do not believe in insects.

Look At This Picture

1 Write down any words that describe what you see.

e.g. green, drops, leaves, circle, spring, tropical

2 Take a word from the list you've just made. Think of any other words you associate with it, any words that come into your head.

e.g. **drops:** *diamonds, drips, sparkle, wet, glass, magnifying*

leaves: *circle shape, spokes of a wheel, fan*

3 Next try to write a short poem or sentence using these words:

The leaves fan out,

Spokes on a wheel,

Spinning wet glass,

like diamonds.

4 You can give your piece of writing a title if you like.

Now You Try It ...

Now you try these four steps with one
of the pictures below or overleaf:

See Me!
See Others!
What Do You See?

THEMED POETRY

This section has three parts:

- ### See Me!
  These are poems about how people see themselves.

- ### See Others!
  These poems make us think about how we judge others.

- ### What Do You See?
  These are poems about imagination and the supernatural.

Awakening

Dorothy Jenkinson

Last week she was one of the gang,
Playing football with the boys,
Tousle-haired
And indistinguishable
From all the rest.
To-day she stands in front of the mirror,
Combing her shampoo-shining locks,
Wondering if Peter really meant it
When he told her she had nice eyes.

POETIC TECHNIQUE:
When lots of words in a poem start with the same letter, it is called **alliteration**.

DIVE IN!

1. What type of person is the girl at the beginning of this poem?

2. How has she changed by the end of the poem?

3. How do you know she has changed? Pick a line from the poem that proves your point.

4. Can you find an example of **alliteration** in this poem?

TAKE THE PLUNGE!

5. Why do you think this poem is called 'Awakening'? What exactly has woken the girl up? What's the big deal?
P Q E

WHY DON'T YOU...

In pairs, imagine it is the next day. The girl goes out to play football looking different. She meets Peter. Continue to write out the conversation they have:

Girl: *(giggles and blushes)* Hi Peter!

Peter: Howya. Get in goal would ya?

Girl: *(flicks hair)* I never play in goal
…

Act out your dialogue for the class.

THRASH IT OUT!

Who tries harder to act cool – boys or girls? (Remember Peter did tell her she had nice eyes!)

®

The Ugly Child

E. Jennings

I heard them say I'm ugly.
I hoped it wasn't true.
I looked into the mirror
To get a better view,
And certainly my face seemed
Uninteresting and sad.
I wish that either it was good
Or else just very bad.

My eyes are green, my hair is straight,
My ears stick out, my nose
Has freckles on it all the year,
I'm skinny as a hose.
If only I could look as I
Imagine I might be.
Oh, all the crowds would turn and bow.
They don't – because I'm me.

1. Why does the child's face in this poem appear 'uninteresting and sad'?

2. Why does the child want to look different?

3. Do you think the child really is ugly?

4. What does he compare himself to?

5. The child thinks that people don't see him because of the way he looks. What is it he wants them to see?

6. How do you think he could make people see the real him?

7. Is it easy to get people to see the 'real' you?

Look at the pictures on the right. In their day these people were considered exceptionally beautiful. Do you think that they are beautiful? Explain your answer fully.

Bring in pictures of three people that you think are beautiful. Does everyone in the class agree? Can you write a definition of beauty?

Maybe 'Beauty is in the eye of the beholder.' ®

OR

Find a song or a movie that deals with the theme of people seeing beyond appearances and bring it into class.

What people say about our appearance affects all of us. Should it? Should people make judgements based on your hair, clothes or accent?

Hairstyle

John Agard

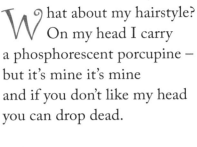

What about my hairstyle?
On my head I carry
a phosphorescent porcupine –
but it's mine it's mine
and if you don't like my head
you can drop dead.

What about my hairstyle?
On my head I bear a mane
of flaming dreadlocks
sometimes hidden by the red
   gold and green
but flaming all the same
with I-rie pride of Africa.
Know what I mean?

phosphorescent –
bright luminous
colour

I-rie –
slang for 'alright'

Incandescent –
shining brightly

What about my hairstyle?
On my head I wear
a Mohican rainbow
that makes me glow.
I know some eyebrows go
up in despair
but it's my hair it's my hair.

What about my hairstyle?
On my head I show a crown
of incandescent candy floss.
Who cares if some people frown
and say, 'Young people are lost'.
At least me Mum doesn't get on me back;
she says, 'I suppose you're only young once.'

What about my hairstyle?
On my head I have whispers
of braided beads.
Me Mum says she wouldn't have the patience –
but theses beads are in no hurry
I tell them my needs
they listen to the song inside of me.

1. What colour and style of hair does the person in the first verse have?

2. In the second verse what does the speaker sometimes hide his dreadlocks with?

3. How do people react to the person with the Mohican hairstyle?

4. Does the person with 'candy floss' hair have a strict mother?

5. Why does the speaker in the fifth verse like their hair?

TAKE THE PLUNGE!

6. All the verses begin with 'What about my hairstyle?' Choose a word from one of the following to describe the tone of this question. Explain your choice. **PQE**

   puzzled, angry, defiant, aggressive, humorous

7. Each of the speakers compares their hairstyle to something. Which comparison was your favourite and why? **PQE**

8. Why do you think these people consider their hairstyles important? **PQE**

9. Reread the last two verses and describe the type of relationship you think these speakers have with their mothers. **PQE**

10. If you had to choose one of these hairstyles, which one would you like and why?

THRASH IT OUT!

In groups, read the quote in the yellow box and try to decide if you agree with it. Give reasons for your answer.

WHY DON'T YOU...

Look at the following photographs of items that have all been in fashion at different times.

What about my piercings?

What about my tattoos?

What about my afro?

What about my flares?

- Imagine you are one of these people and write three verses starting with one of the captions under the pictures.

- See if you can use metaphors like the writer of this poem.

OR

Write a letter of complaint from the school to the parents of one of the people in the poem. Check out the example on page 176.

'The young people of today love luxury. They have bad manners, they scoff at authority and lack respect for their elders. Children nowadays are really tyrants, they no longer stand up when their elders come into the room where they are sitting, they contradict their parents, chat together in the presence of adults, eat gluttonously and tyrannise their teachers.'

Check the date this was written at the bottom of page 137.

Were you surprised to see how long ago this was written?

135

Back in the Playground Blues

Adrian Mitchell

Dreamed I was in a school playground,
    I was about four feet high
Yes dreamed I was back in the playground,
    and standing about four feet high
The playground was three miles long and the
    playground was five miles wide
It was broken black tarmac with a high fence
    all around
Broken black dusty tarmac with a high fence
    running all around
And it had a special name to it, they called it
    The Killing Ground.

Got a mother and a father, they're a thousand miles away
The Rulers of the Killing Ground are coming out to play
Everyone thinking: who are they going to play with today

    You get it for being Jewish
    Get it for being black
    Get it for being chicken
    Get it for fighting back
    You get it for being big and fat
    Get it for being small
    Oh those who get it get it and get it
    For any damn thing at all

Sometimes they take a beetle, tear off its six legs one by one
Beetle on its black back rocking in the lunchtime sun
But a beetle can't beg for mercy, a beetle's not half the fun
Heard a deep voice talking, it had the iceberg sound
'It prepares them for life' – but I have never found
Any place in my life that's worse than the Killing Ground.

1. How does the title of this poem let you know that it is not going to be happy?

2. In the first verse, how do you know that the dream the poet is describing is actually a nightmare?

3. What tells us that the poet feels helpless at the start of the second verse?

4. Who do the rulers of 'The Killing Ground' pick on?

5. What do they do to the beetle?

6. Why do you think the playground was called 'The Killing Ground'? **P Q E**

7. Why doesn't the adult help the children in the final verse? **P Q E**

8. Does the grown-up poet agree or disagree with this attitude, in your opinion?

Read the following poem:

Name-calling

Charles Thomson

They called me frog-face with ears like a bat.
I said, 'I'm not – I'm worse than that.'

They called me rat-nose with a tongue like a shoe.
I said, 'Is that the best you can do?'

They called me mouse-eyes, skunk-breath, dog-head.
I said, 'I'm worse than all you've said.'

They said, 'It's no fun calling you a name.'
I called, 'That's a pity – I'm enjoying this game.'

Imagine Charles Thomson is giving the young Adrian Mitchell advice. In pairs write the conversation between the two children.

OR

Draw a picture of the playground described in 'Back in the Playground Blues'.

In groups write a list of five things you can do if you are being bullied.

Socrates, 400 B.C.

137

See Others!

Exile

Moniza Alvi

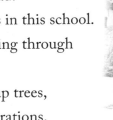

The old land swinging in her stomach
she must get to know this language
better – key words, sound patterns
word groups of fire and blood.

Try your classmates with
the English version of your name.
Maria. Try it.
Good afternoon. How are you?

I am fine. Your country –
you see it in a drop of water.
The last lesson they taught you there
was how to use a gun.

And now in stops and starts
you grow a second
city in your head.
It is Christmas in this school.
Sarajevo is falling through

a forest of lit-up trees,
cards and decorations.
Mountains split with gunfire
swallow clouds, birds, sky.

1. Who is speaking in this poem?
2. Where do you think she is from?
3. Why is she not in her own country?
4. Do you know what the word 'exile' means?
5. What is the girl trying to learn?
6. What did she learn in the past?

7. What is the poet trying to describe for the reader in the first line?
8. Two different Christmases are described. Can you explain the difference in your own words?
9. Why does the poet use the **metaphor** 'fire and blood' when talking about the girl's new language?
10. Have you ever been homesick? Write a short description of how it felt.

Imagine that you have been told that a bomb is about to explode in your city in five minutes' time. You have that much time to gather your most valuable belongings and leave. What would you bring and why? ®

POETIC TECHNIQUE:
When the poet creates an image by comparing two things of different natures, without using the words 'like', 'as' or 'than', it is called a **metaphor**.

Luck in Sarajevo

Izet Sarajlić

In Sarajevo
in the spring of 1992,
everything is possible:

you go stand in a bread line
and end up in an emergency room
with your leg amputated.

Afterwards, you still maintain
that you were very lucky.

What do you think of this person's attitude to luck?

In groups, choose one of the following scenarios about good or bad luck:

- You are a poor family who have just won the Lotto

- You are an Olympic athlete who has tripped in the relay race, just as your team was about to win the gold medal

- You are archaeologists who have just discovered buried treasure

POETIC TECHNIQUE:

A **freeze-frame** is like a scene from a film that has been paused. You decide what character each person is playing. Choose a moment from their story, and 'freeze' the action that is taking place. Remember to think about posture, gesture, expression and positions.

Pick one of these scenarios and compose a *freeze-frame*.

First, decide who each person is and what moment you are describing.

Then practise your moment.

The teacher will call each group to the top of the classroom in turn.

On the count of three you must freeze your moment and hold it still for thirty seconds.

When the teacher points to you, you must explain:

- Who you are

- How you feel. What are your hopes and fears?

Tonight, write a short diary entry based on the experiences of your character.

No Sheep !

Your Poets are STUPID !

The People of the Other Village

Thomas Lux

hate the people of this village

and would nail our hats

to our heads for refusing in their presence to remove them

or staple our hands to our foreheads

for refusing to salute them

if we did not hurt them first: mail them packages of rats,

mix their flour at night with broken glass.

We do this, they do that.

They peel the larynx from one of our brothers' throats.

We devein one of their sisters.

The quicksand pits they built were good.

Our amputation teams were better.

We trained some birds to steal their wheat.

They sent us exploding ambassadors of peace.

They do this, we do that.

We canceled our sheep imports.

They no longer bought our blankets.

We mocked their greatest poet

and when that had no effect

we parodied the way they dance

which did cause pain, so they, in turn, said our God

was leprous, hairless.

We do this, they do that.

Ten thousand (10,000) years, ten thousand

(10,000) brutal, beautiful years.

No Saluting

devein —
remove veins

parodied —
made fun of

Your God is HAIRLESS !

No Blankets !

140

1. Why do you think 'The People of the Other Village hate the people of this village'?

2. In your opinion, what is the worst thing the people do to each other in this poem?

3. What do you think is the most ridiculous thing they do?

4. Do you think these people really hate each other, or is this poem more about fear? Explain your answer fully. **PQE**

5. The poet uses exaggeration. Why?

6. What do you think is the main **theme** of this poem? **PQE**

POETIC TECHNIQUE:

The **theme** of a poem is the main topic or issue in the poem.

Imagine you are running for election in one of these villages. Design a poster or write a speech, outlining your plans for the enemy. You must convince the people of your village that you will do a good job if elected.

First They Came for the Jews
Pastor Niemöller

First they came for the Jews
and I did not speak out –
because I was not a Jew.
Then they came for the communists
and I did not speak out –
because I was not a communist.
Then they came for the trade unionists
and I did not speak out –
because I was not a trade unionist.
Then they came for me –
and there was no one left
to speak out for me.

1. What do you think the speaker in this poem is trying to explain to you?

2. Who do you think 'they' are?

This poem is written by an Aboriginal Australian.

Never Blood So Red

Grandfather Koori

Never blood
so red so red
never blood so red
as blood of the poet
the Kokatha poet
who lay in the pool
so dead.
Never blood
so red so red
in Fremantle gaol so red
it glistens on batons
walls and feet
red drops on the warden's head
never blood
so red so red
never blood so red
as blood of the poet
the Kokatha poet
whose cries for justice
bled
whose cries for justice
bled.

1. What do you think happens in this poem?

2. What words are repeated? Why do you think this is?

Split into groups and read this poem out loud. Try to think of ways of emphasising the beat.

Maybe you could:

- Read a line each

- Shout certain words or phrases

- Read some words together and some words alone

- Add sound effects

Try to capture the aggression and violence in your voices.

- Divide into groups and discuss situations when it is important to speak out.

  Try to think of examples
  - in your own life
  - your country
  - the world.

- Do you think there are times when it is wiser to stay silent?

- Should everyone be entitled to voice their opinion?

- Choose a chairperson who will report the three most important points back to the class.

- After you have listened to all the groups' points, write a report on the class' findings.

Not Waving But Drowning

Stevie Smith

Nobody heard him, the dead man,
   But still he lay moaning:
I was much further out than you thought
And not waving but drowning.

Poor chap, he always loved larking
And now he's dead
It must have been too cold for him his
heart gave way,
They said.

Oh, no no no, it was too cold always
(Still the dead one lay moaning)
I was much too far out all my life
And not waving but drowning.

DIVE IN!

1. Look at the title of the poem. What do you think the poet is trying to say?

2. How did people think the 'poor chap' had died?

3. Why does he think he died?

WHY DON'T YOU...

Look at the picture accompanying this poem. It is a famous painting by Edward Munch called *The Scream*. Write a description of how the person in the painting is feeling.

OR

Draw your own picture to illustrate the poem.

TAKE THE PLUNGE!

4. Do you notice any examples of **assonance** in the poem? What effect do they have?

5. Reread the last verse and decide what the poem is really about. What is the *theme* of the poem?

POETIC TECHNIQUE:
When a vowel sound is repeated in a line, it is called **assonance**.

144

The Butterfly

Margit Koretzová

Imagine you are a judge in an art competition. How many marks would you give this painting, and why?

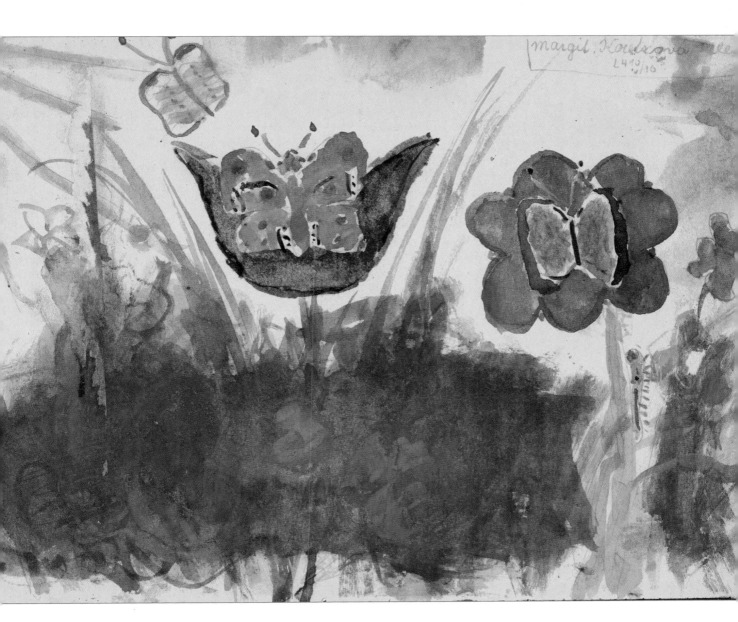

When you have finished discussing the painting, look across the page …

The Butterfly

Pavel Friedman

The last, the very last,
So richly, brightly, dazzlingly yellow.
Perhaps if the sun's tears would sing
Against a white stone …

Such, such a yellow
Is carried lightly way up high.
It went away I'm sure because it wished
to kiss the world goodbye.

For seven weeks I've lived in here,
Penned up inside this ghetto
But I have found my people here.
The dandelions call to me
And the white chestnut candles in the court.
Only I never saw another butterfly.

That butterfly was the last one.
Butterflies don't live in here,
In the ghetto.

Margit Koretzová was deported by the Nazis to the 'holding centre' of Terezin ghetto in Czechoslovakia, on 17 January 1942. She was moved to Auschwitz where she died in 1944. She was 11 years old. She drew the butterfly painting while she was in Terezin. Pavel Friedman was also held in Terezin. He died at the age of 23 in Auschwitz.

1. Why do you think the poet says the butterfly is 'so richly, brightly, dazzlingly yellow'?

2. Why don't butterflies live in the ghetto?

3. Does knowing about the painter and the poet change the way you feel about the picture and poem? Explain your answer fully.

4. How did the poem make you feel? Pick a line that made you feel this way.

Find out more about Terezin and Auschwitz. You can find information in your history books, on the internet, in the library, or by asking parents or teachers.

Happiness

Carl Sandburg

I ASKED the professors who teach the meaning of life to tell me what is happiness.

And I went to famous executives who boss the work of thousands of men.

They all shook their heads and gave me a smile as though I was trying to fool with them

And then one Sunday afternoon I wandered out along the Desplaines river

And I saw a crowd of Hungarians under the trees with their women and children and a keg of beer and an accordion.

1. Who did the poet go to to find out about happiness?

2. Could they give him an answer?

3. Does he find out what happiness is?

4. Do you think the poem has a good title? Give reasons for your answer.

5. Do you think the poet himself is happy?

Remember one of the happiest moments in your life and try to describe it in one sentence.

OR

Interview three people you admire to find out their definition of happiness.

OR

Bring in a song that always puts you in a good mood. Play it for the class and explain why it makes you happy.

What Do You See?
What's That Down There?

Adrian Mitchell

What's that down there?
What's that moving?
What's that moving down in the dark
of this chilly black maze of a cave?

Is it Sarallo –
The scarlet snake with the seven
Silver heads
And fangs that snap like a murder trap?

What's that down there?
What's that moving?
What's that moving down in the dark
of this chilly black maze of a cave?

Is it Farranaway –
That back-cracking brute
With a hundred horns
And hoofs that hit like horrible hammers?

What's that down there?
What's that moving?
What's that moving down in the dark
of this chilly black maze of a cave?

Is it Thilissa –
That slippery wisp of
A whispering ghost of a
Girl who died
In the moistness of mist
Which lies like a shroud on
The underground lake
down in the dark in this chilly black maze of a cave?

DIVE IN!

1. What do you think of the opening of this poem?

2. Which image was your favourite?

3. Pick as many 'sound' words as you can find in the poem.

4. Certain words appeal to your sense of touch. Can you find any?

TAKE THE PLUNGE!

5. The poet uses **alliteration** to create atmosphere. Find as many examples as you can.

6. There is also **onomatopoeia** in this poem. Can you find it?

POETIC TECHNIQUE:

When a word imitates the sound it is describing, it is called **onomatopoeia**.

WHY DON'T YOU ...

Draw a picture from this poem.

OR

Write an essay beginning ...

It was a dark and stormy night. Three men sat in a cave. One man said to the other, 'Tell us a story' ...

THRASH IT OUT!

Does anyone in your class know a good ghost story?

OR

Bring in a copy of the animated film *Monsters, Inc.* Watch the first ten minutes of the film in class. Divide into groups and discuss the film under the following headings:

- How was the opening scene surprising?

- What is unusual about the monsters' world?

- How is the film trying to change our view of monsters?

- If you have not seen the film, would you like to see the rest of it? Why?

- If you *have* seen the film, did you enjoy it? Why?

For homework, write a brief review of the opening scenes of *Monsters, Inc.*

Blood Is an Acquired Taste

Roger McGough

Blood is an acquired taste
'tis warm and sickly
and sticks to the teeth
a surfeit makes me puke.
I judge my victims as a connoisseur
a sip here, a mouthful there.
I never kill
and am careful to cause no pain
to those who sleeping nourish me
and calling once I never call again.

So if one morning you awake,
stretch, and remember
dark dreams of
　　falling
　　　falling
if your neck is sore
a mark that wasn't there the night before
be not afeard 'tis but a sign
I give thee thanks
I have drunk thy wine.

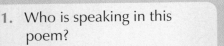

DIVE IN!

1. Who is speaking in this poem?

2. Do you think the speaker is a pleasant character? Make a list of his positive and negative qualities.

3. What kind of attitude does the speaker have towards his victims?

TAKE THE PLUNGE!

4. What kind of language does the speaker use? P Q E

5. Some of the descriptions in this poem are very *visceral*. This means that they are stomach-churning. What words do you think are visceral? P Q E

6. Look at the second verse. What do you notice about the shape of the words on the page? Why do you think the poet did this?

Make a list of as many vampire characters as you can think of. Say which one is your favourite and why.

OR

Write a poem from the point of view of one of the following:

- Monster
- Witch
- Troll
- Giant
- Werewolf
- Warlock
- Goblin
- Zombie

OR

Design your own film poster and movie title like the example shown here.

Write down your opinion of the following statement:

Horror stories and films are an unpleasant waste of time.

Have a class discussion based on your answers. Write a brief summary of the main points at the end.

Don't worry if you don't understand all the words in the extract, just concentrate on getting the gist of it.

Macbeth
The Witches

William Shakespeare

Round about the cauldron go;
In the poison'd entrails throw.
Toad that under cold stone
Days and nights hast thirty-one
Swelter'd venom sleeping got,
Boil thou first i' the charmed pot.
    Double, double toil and trouble;
    Fire burn and cauldron bubble.
Fillet of a fenny snake,
In the cauldron boil and bake;
Eye of newt, and toe of frog,
Wool of bat, and tongue of dog,
Adder's fork, and blind-worm's sting,
Lizard's leg, and howlet's wing,
For a charm of powerful trouble,
Like a hell-broth boil and bubble
    Double, double toil and trouble;
    Fire burn and cauldron bubble.

Scale of dragon, tooth of wolf,
Witch's mummy, maw and gulf
Of the ravin'd salt-sea shark,
Root of hemlock digg'd i' the dark,
Liver of blaspheming Jew,
Gall of goat, and slips of yew
Silver'd in the moon's eclipse,
Nose of Turk, and Tartar's lips,
Finger of birth-strangled babe
Ditch-delivered by a drab,
Make the gruel thick and slab;
Add thereto a tiger's chaudron
For the ingredients of our cauldron.
    Double, double toil and trouble;
    Fire burn and cauldron bubble.
Cool it with a baboon's blood,
Then the charm is firm and good.

TAKE THE PLUNGE!

1. Rewrite this extract as if it were a recipe in a modern cookery book. List the main ingredients, and the amounts, followed by instructions.

2. Write some spells that would help you to:

   - Take over the world
   - Get a boyfriend/girlfriend
   - Cure baldness
   - Succeed at exams
   - Become popular

3. Imagine that you meet the three women in the photo on the opposite page. Write a story about what happens.

WHY DON'T YOU...

Read this aloud in groups of three, and maybe act it out.

OR

Make a rap version of the witches' spell (you could add beats or sound effects).

The Mewlips

J.R.R. Tolkien

The shadows where the Mewlips dwell
Are dark and wet as ink,
And slow and softly rings their bell,
As in the slime you sink.

You sink into the slime, who dare
To knock upon their door,
While down the grinning gargoyles stare
And noisome waters pour.

Beside the rotting river-strand
The dropping willows weep,
And gloomily the gorcrows stand
Croaking in their sleep.

Over the Merlock Mountains a long and
 weary way,
In a mouldy valley where the trees are grey,
By a dark pool's borders without wind or
 tide,
Moonless and sunless, where the
 Mewlips hide.

The cellars where the Mewlips sit
Are deep and dank and cold
With single sickly candle lit;
And there they count their gold.

Their walls are wet, their ceilings drip;
Their feet upon the floor
Go softly with a squish-flap-flip,
As they sidle to the door.

They peep out slyly; through a crack
Their feeling fingers creep,
And when they've finished, in a sack
Your bones they take to keep.

Beyond the Merlock Mountains, a long and
 lonely road.
Through the spider-shadows and the
 marsh of Tode.
Through the wood of hanging trees and
 the gallows-weed,
You go to find the Mewlips – and the
 Mewlips feed.

DIVE IN!

1. Would you like to visit the Mewlips? Give a reason for your answer.

2. Pick out three lines in the poem that you think best describe the **atmosphere.**

WHY DON'T YOU...

Write a description of one of the following places, creating as distinctive an **atmosphere** as you can:

- A windswept beach
- A city fountain
- A garden shed
- A school library
- An opera concert
- An operating theatre
- A desert
- A ghost town
- A mountain top
- A funfair house of horrors

155

3

Read All About It!

In this chapter you will learn about:

- Newspapers
- Advertising
- Formal letter writing
- Report writing

THE IRISH TIMES

BUDGET 2010
PAT McARDLE ON WHAT WE SHOULD EXPECT THIS AFTERNOON   PAGE 18

STUDENT STRESS

MASTER OF THE TURF
BRIAN O'CONNOR ON THE CAREER OF PACK SUNANE Sports Wednesday

NewsDigest

Gardaí warned on industrial action

Saudi government plans to open school in Dublin

HomeNews

Lenihan says spending cuts will be focus of the budget

Minister forecasts it will be last 'of the very difficult budgets'

Herald angola: children attend opening of live animal crib at Mansion House

Fallout from child abuse report to dominate meeting of bishops

Cartier

temperatures ate summit

Report on Local Fundraising Project

Introduction
The Chernobyl Children's Project asked the community to get involved in fundraising for the orphans in Belarus. The community decided to fill a container truck with goods to be transported to Belarus. Donations of clothes, dry goods, blankets, medical supplies and toys were requested.

Information
A container truck was parked in the car park of MacCarthy's Supermarket for the duration of the project. Over the course of two weeks, people were encouraged to drop off goods between 10 am and 10 pm. A rota of volunteers was set up in order to receive, sort and pack the goods. Other volunteers put up posters to raise awareness of the project. An enormous volume of goods was received, mostly of very high quality. Many people bought goods in the supermarket for donation. The busiest drop-off times were early in the morning, lunchtime and early in the evening. Other times were very quiet.

Conclusion
From observation of the project, the generosity of many people is clear. However, a minority of people took the opportunity to clean out their attics, and contributed worthless and broken items. It was felt that there was not enough publicity, and that the posters were unclear, particularly about drop-off times. It was difficult to find enough volunteers to man the container truck for the full day.

Recommendations
Due to these conclusions, it is recommended that, in future, the following steps be taken for a project of this type:

1) Material should be sorted inappr
2) Public newsle involv
3) Drop-o Findin

SUNSILK

'Deeply Brunette to awaken & enhance a deeper colour'

SUNSILK
Deeply Brunette

CHERYL

'Seeing Red'

adidas.com

adidas

Before you begin this chapter, bring in a newspaper from home, or ask your local shop for one of yesterday's unsold newspapers.

Have you noticed that there's more than one kind of newspaper?

BROADSHEETS and TABLOIDS

A **broadsheet** is a 'quality' newspaper with serious and in-depth reporting on a wide range of important issues. It is A2 size. It uses formal language and tries to give the facts without exaggerating.

A **tabloid** newspaper reports mostly on scandals, gossip and celebrities, in a sensational style. It is A3 size, which is half the size of a broadsheet. It uses simple, exaggerated language and slang.

 Draw two columns in your copybook. Write the word 'Tabloid' at the top of one and 'Broadsheet' at the top of the other. Look at the following phrases and words and see if you can put them in pairs under the correct headings.

NUTCASE!

YOB

FLOP

GARDA

SUSPECTED MURDERER

CANCELLED

NARCOTICS OPERATION

SCRAPPED

COPS

PSYCHO KILLER

MENTALLY-ILL PATIENT

DRUGS SWOOP

FAILURE

UNCOUTH YOUTH

Front Pages

The first part of the newspaper that you see is the front page. This has to be **eye-catching** to convince you to buy the paper. Newspapers use different tricks to attract our attention. You can tell the difference between a tabloid and a broadsheet at a glance.

BROADSHEET

Masthead
the name of the paper (black on white)

Article
written in columns

Second front page story

Contents list
tells you where to find stories in the paper

Banner headline
for main article

Caption

Photo
to illustrate an article

Advertisement

TABLOID

Masthead
the name of the paper (red and white)

More of the page is used for **headlines** *in the tabloid*

Lead article
very short

Sports story advertised

Big headline
dramatic and sensational

Photo
to illustrate an article

Make a list of the similarities and differences that you can see in these two examples. Now bring in some front-page examples from today's newspapers and see if you can identify the main features. Swap them around the class.

Headlines

Headlines tell you what a newspaper story is about:

- Broadsheets use <u>informative</u>, <u>serious</u> language:

  e.g. *DPP cites time-limit constraint in garda complaints.*

- Tabloids use <u>sensational</u> and <u>exaggerated</u> language:

  e.g. *Frantic hunt for lone knife raider.*

Tabloids also use **puns** and **alliteration** to make their headlines eye-catching.

Puns

When people play with words that sound similar or that mean the same thing, in order to be funny, it is called a 'pun'. For example:

WINDS MEAN THIS WON'T BE A BREEZE
(heavy winds make sailing race difficult)

BJÖRN FREE
(Tennis player Björn Borg free of injury)

MATCH GETS CARLOW DOWN
(Carlow beaten 22–2 by Down)

Alliteration

Headlines often repeat the same letter to make them sound powerful. For example:

TAX <u>H</u>IKE <u>H</u>ORROR

MINISTER <u>B</u>LAMES <u>B</u>AD <u>B</u>UDGET

<u>B</u>ECKHAM <u>B</u>IDS <u>B</u>YE-<u>B</u>YE

Write a tabloid and a broadsheet headline to accompany each of the following stories:

OR

- A murder suspect is held for questioning by Gardaí
- New gorilla delivered to the zoo
- Surprise defeat for famous sporting team
- Scandal as government minister takes bribe
- New breakthrough in cancer research
- Residents protest the noise levels from rock concert
- Storm at sea claims 12 lives
- Irish song wins Eurovision
- Famous boy band breaks up
- Prehistoric fossil, found in New Zealand, proves humans descended from spiders

Rewrite the following tabloid headlines as broadsheet headlines:

GOVERNMENT JET IS SCRAPPED

PSYCHO KILLER ON THE PROWL

VICIOUS MUGGER ATTACKS GRANNY

SUNNY SUNDAY SWIM TURNS DEADLY

SHAME OF SOCCER CHEAT

From the newspapers in the classroom, pick out three headlines from a broadsheet and three from a tabloid. Explain how you know which is which.

Rewrite the following broadsheet headlines as tabloid headlines:

Poor forecast threatens potato crop

New study shows mobile phone usage on increase

Educational disadvantage remains untackled

Judge issues stern warning to drunk driver

Transfer rumour denied by United manager

Reports

CROKER COUNTDOWN: Three days to U2's homecoming party

'WE'LL GIVE OUR BANDS €5M EDGE'

U2 invest in hopefuls

GET SET: U2's 'Claw' stage being erected yesterday for their Croke Park shows

■ By KATHRYN ROGERS

ROCK giants U2 are donating a whopping €5 million to provide music training to budding Irish stars.

The multi-million euro fund will go towards teaching young people to play an instrument or have their voice trained.

According to the Edge, the band had been "looking for some time for a way to get involved in an initiative in music education in Ireland".

"Being around music at a young age was important for us and we were lucky to have it at school," he said.

Charity

The monies will be rolled out between 2010 and 2015, and will be administered by non-profit organisation Music Network it U2 — who play Croke Park this Friday, Saturday and Monday — decided they should "get behind" the Music Network scheme.

International charity The Ireland Funds will also finance the scheme, and will begin a campaign to raise another €2m.

The following two reports are describing the same event. One is from a tabloid, the other from a broadsheet. Read them both.

Article from the Irish Daily Star:

'WE'LL GIVE OUR BANDS €5M EDGE'

U2 invest in hopefuls

by **Kathryn Rogers**

Rock giants U2 are donating a whopping €5 million to provide music training to budding Irish stars.

The multi-million euro fund will go towards teaching young people to play an instrument or have their voice trained.

According to the Edge, the band had been "looking for some time for a way to get involved in an initiative in music education in Ireland".

Charity

"Being around music at a young age was important for us and we were lucky to have it at school," he said.

The monies will be rolled out between 2010 and 2015, and will be administered by non-profit organisation Music Network.

U2 — who play Croke Park this Friday, Saturday and Monday — decided they should "get behind" the Music Network scheme.

International charity The Ireland Funds will also finance the scheme, and will begin a campaign to raise another €2m.

U2 to give €5m for music tuition

ROCK BAND U2 are to contribute €5 million to a new music training fund for children which is aimed at redressing inequality in music education in Ireland.

The Ireland Funds international charity is also giving its backing to the scheme which aims to teach young people to play a musical instrument or to have their voice trained.

Deirdre McCrea, chief executive of non-profit organisation Music Network, which is administering the fund, said: "It is currently very inequitable that the opportunity to play music depends on your parents' ability to afford that privilege, to buy musical instruments and to drive you to lessons."

U2 guitarist the Edge said: "Being around music at a young age was important for us and we were lucky to have it at school."

The band had been "looking for some time for a way to get involved in an initiative in music education in Ireland, he said in a statement. After speaking to various people about what to do, the band thought the scheme was "really well thought out" and that they should "get behind it".

The Ireland Funds will also part-finance the scheme and is beginning a campaign to raise €2 million.

Ireland Funds chief executive Kingsley Aikens said there was a gap that had to be filled in this area for a country with such a reputation for music.

Mr Aikens was referring to 2003 research by the Music Network which revealed that only 1 per cent of children of secondary school age received tuition in instrumental or vocal performance compared with 6 to 8 per cent in other EU countries.

Mr Aikens said he hoped that the Government would continue the scheme, but he was unable to get any guarantees yet.

GENEVIEVE CARBERY

Article from the Irish Times:

U2 to give €5m for music tuition

GENEVIEVE CARBERY

ROCK BAND U2 are to contribute €5 million to a new music training fund for children which is aimed at redressing inequality in music education in Ireland.

The Ireland Funds international charity is also giving its backing to the scheme which aims to teach young people to play a musical instrument or to have their voice trained.

Deirdre McCrea, chief executive of non-profit organisation Music Network, which is administering the fund, said: "It is currently very inequitable that the opportunity to play music depends on your parents' ability to afford that privilege, to buy musical instruments and to drive you to lessons."

U2 guitarist the Edge said: "Being around music at a young age was important for us and we were lucky to have it at school."

The band had been "looking for some time for a way to get involved in an initiative in music education in Ireland," he said in a statement. After speaking to various people about what to do, the band thought the scheme was "really well thought out" and that they should "get behind it".

The Ireland Funds will also part-finance the scheme and is beginning a campaign to raise €2 million.

Ireland Funds chief executive Kingsley Aikens said there was a gap that had to be filled in this area for a country with such a reputation for music.

Mr Aikens was referring to 2003 research by the Music Network which revealed that only 1 per cent of children of secondary school age received tuition in instrumental or vocal performance compared with 6 to 8 per cent in other EU countries.

Mr Aikens said he hoped that the Government would continue the scheme, but he was unable to get any guarantees yet.

From these reports find the answers to the following questions:

- **WHAT** happened?
- **WHO** was involved?
- **WHERE** did it happen?
- **WHEN** did it happen?
- **WHY** did it happen?
- **HOW** did it happen?

The Inverted Pyramid

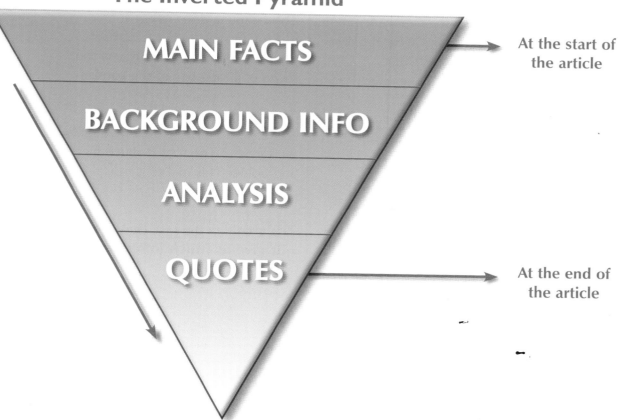

MAIN FACTS — At the start of the article

BACKGROUND INFO

ANALYSIS

QUOTES — At the end of the article

You have just established what journalists call the **inverted pyramid**. This is the structure they use to write reports.

Spot the Differences

Front Page Article from the *Irish Times* (broadsheet)	Front Page Article from the *Irish Daily Star* (tabloid)
## U2 to give €5m for music tuition	## 'WE'LL GIVE OUR BANDS €5M EDGE'
This headline names the famous Irish rock band. It clearly states what the band intends to do with €5 million.	This headline does not give as much information but it is **more dramatic** because it contains the name of a member of the band.
The **print** used in the *Irish Times* headline is black writing on a white backgound.	The **print** used in the *Irish Daily Star* is white writing on a black/grey background. The font is much bigger and bolder. This makes it more eye-catching.
The *Irish Times* article is **highly researched.** This is evident in the **detailed information** provided regarding the two organisations which are going to administer the fund. It also refers to statistical research.	The article in the *Irish Daily Star* **does not give as much information**.
This article is **neutral** and **unbiased.** It does not exaggerate the facts.	The *Irish Daily Star* article uses more **sensational language**. For example it calls U2 **'rock giants'** and it uses the word **'whopping'** to describe the €5m.
There is **no photograph** provided alongside the *Irish Times* article.	The tabloid article includes **two photographs**, one photo is of U2's 'claw stage', the other is a **close-up** photograph of Bono, the lead singer of the band.

Stylistic Features

Features of Broadsheets

Layout and Content

Cover important global and national stories

Cover stories on politics, finance and current affairs

Headlines

Informative

Factual

Serious language

Black print on white

U2 to give €5m for music tuition

Reports and Articles

Highly researched

Factual details

Neutral and unbiased

Few quotations

Few photographs

Small print

Features of Tabloids

Layout and Content

Cover sensational news

Cover stories about scandals, gossip, celebrities and sport

Headlines

Dramatic

Exaggerated

Use of slang

Bold and colour print

'WE'LL GIVE OUR BANDS €5M EDGE'

Reports and Articles

Some research

Less factual details, more speculation

Bias obvious

Many quotations

Large, eye-catching photographs

Large print

WHY DON'T YOU...

Compose a headline, write a report (tabloid or broadsheet) and lay out a front page article for one of the following news items.

- An important building, local or national, has been destroyed by a fire

- An extremely valuable item has been stolen

- Freak weather disrupts the country

- An assassination attempt on an important public figure

- A major sporting event

Advertising

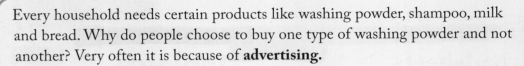

Every household needs certain products like washing powder, shampoo, milk and bread. Why do people choose to buy one type of washing powder and not another? Very often it is because of **advertising.**

The purpose of an advertisement is to **persuade** us, the consumers (the people who buy things), that we *need* a product or service. In order to persuade us, the creators of ads target specific groups. They won't try to sell mortgages to a group of thirteen year olds, but they will try to sell them mobile phones! These specific groups are known as the **target audience**.

Conduct a survey at home tonight.

1 DIVIDE ... the class into groups.

2 ASSIGN ... each group one of the following times to watch the ads that appear on the television.

- 5.00 p.m. RTÉ 2
- 7.15 p.m. TV3
- 9.15 p.m. RTÉ 1
- 6.15 p.m. RTÉ 1
- 8.45 p.m. Network 2

3 BASED ... on the ads that appear, can you guess who the advertisers think is watching television at that time?

4 WRITE ... down who you believe to be the main **target audience** for these ads.

5 COMPILE ... your results tomorrow in class.

Visuals

Advertisers use photographs, pictures, cartoons, colours and graphics to:

Advertising in magazines and newspapers (the print media) contains two elements, visuals and copy (the written part of the ad).

- Show us the product.

- Make us familiar with the product through the use of a **logo** – a symbol used to represent the product, like the Golden Arches of McDonald's or the Nike tick.

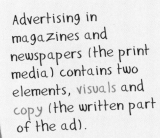

- Make the product seem glamorous.

- Shock us into noticing the product.

- Make us laugh.

- Warn us that bad things will happen to us if we don't use the product.

- Associate the product with someone famous. This is called **endorsement.**

- Appeal to our emotions.

Copy

Any writing in an ad is called copy. This can include:

- **Captions** – the headings in an ad.

- **Slogans** – repeated catchphrases associated with the product.

- **Buzz words** – words that the advertisers know will catch your attention like,

FREE! GUARANTEED! NEW! IMPROVED!

- Positive language associated with the product.

- Negative language if you don't have the product.

The design of the writing, or **typography,** also gives us a message about the product.

- The *font* used creates different effects

  e.g. **SPEEDY**, *SPEEDY,* Old Fashioned, **Old Fashioned**

- The *colour* of the print also sends a message e.g. red for excitement, blue for calm.

- The *size* of the print lets us see the most important information first.

Have a look at the ads on the following pages to see how the advertiser has used the visuals and copy.

Ice makes us think of the cold

Caption

Buzz words with positive connotations (innovative, efficient, taken care of)

Typography of logo

Shows us the product

www.indesit.com

New Indesit Fridge Freezers.
Ice and easy does it.

Chill out with a new Indesit fridge freezer. Our Easy Ice feature is an innovative design development that incorporates the ice tray within the freezer door to save space so that you can fit even more food inside. Indesit also offers a No Frost feature that ensures efficient cooling of the freezer contents at all times and means that you never have to defrost again. Everything's cool and taken care of. For a full range brochure, please call 08700 104 309.

(i) INDESIT
We work, you play.

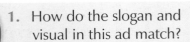

DIVE IN!

1. How do the slogan and visual in this ad match?

2. There is a pun in the caption. Can you find it?

3. Pick out the buzz words from the copy.

WHY DON'T YOU...

Cut out an ad from a magazine at home and analyse it like the ad above, except write out all of the points in proper sentences into your copybook.

DIVE IN!

1. Is this an unusual image for a washing powder ad? Why do you think the advertiser chose it?

2. What does this ad promise?

3. Who do you think this ad is aimed at? Why?

Strawberries and Squirty Whipped Cream.
Stain nos. 81 and 34 of 99.
Surf removes 99 stains. Guaranteed.

BELIEF

Strength

Family

'Seeing Red'

adidas.com

Impossible is nothing

DIVE IN!

1. Why would Adidas pay David Beckham to endorse their product?

2. What message do you think is in the slogan?

3. Identify the Adidas logo and draw it into your copybook.

1. How many colours are used in this ad?

2. Do you think this ad is effective?

3. What information is contained in the copy?

ROCKPORT

FRESH ATTITUDE

Call 01524 591894 for stockists or visit WWW.ROCKPORT.COM

ROCKPORT. AUTHENTIC COMFORT. MODERN STYLE.

Get Fizzical with Stains.

Persil's fizzing action penetrates deep into fibres to remove even the toughest greasy and outdoor stains. For lovely bubbly clean clothes. For a free sample, go to www.persil.com or phone 0800 10 60 14

New Persil Performance

1. Explain the pun in this ad.

2. Pick out as many buzz words as you can.

3. Can you find any examples of alliteration in this ad?

DIVE IN!

1. How does this advertisement catch our attention?

2. What is the slogan and what do you think it means?

3. How does this ad appeal to our emotions?

Danone Actimel. Your daily defence drink.

SUNSILK

'Deeply Brunette to awaken & enhance a deeper colour'

SUNSILK
Deeply Brunette

DIVE IN!

1. Who is this ad aimed at?

2. Why did the advertisers choose this celebrity to market their product?

3. Why is a picture of the product included in the ad?

Formal Letter

A formal letter is a business letter or a letter to someone you don't know. Therefore it must be very polite and written according to specific rules.

Letters of thanks, letters from banks,

Letters of joy from girl and boy,

Receipted bills and invitations

To inspect new stock or to visit relations,

And applications for situations,

And timid lovers' declarations,

And gossip, gossip from all the nations.

From 'Night Mail' by W. H. Auden

You are writing a letter of application for a job as a lifeguard.
Here is the plan you might do beforehand:

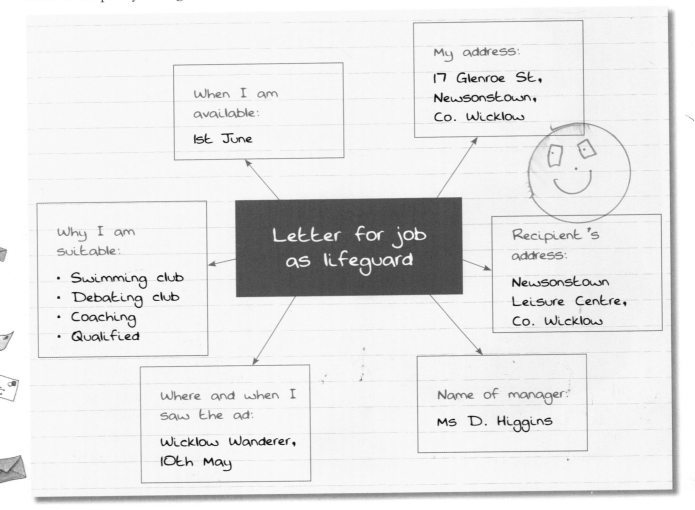

When I am available:

1st June

My address:

17 Glenroe St,
Newsonstown,
Co. Wicklow

Why I am suitable:

- Swimming club
- Debating club
- Coaching
- Qualified

Letter for job as lifeguard

Recipient's address:

Newsonstown Leisure Centre,
Co. Wicklow

Where and when I saw the ad:

Wicklow Wanderer,
10th May

Name of manager:

Ms D. Higgins

17 Glenroe St,
Newsonstown,
Co. Wicklow.

Your address and the date

12th May 2011

Name, position and address of the person you are writing to

Ms D. Higgins,

Manager,

Newsonstown Leisure Centre,

Co. Wicklow.

Greeting

Dear Ms. Higgins, To whom it may concern / Dear Sir/madam.

I am applying for the position of Assistant Lifeguard as advertised in the Wicklow Wanderer on 10th May.

I am seventeen years old and am presently finishing Transition Year in Newsonstown Community School. I am a member of the school's swimming club and am also active in the debating society, which has greatly improved my communication skills.

Information you want the recipient to know

I am used to taking responsibility, as I was senior prefect this year and also accompanied the swimming coach and the junior team to galas. I have completed my lifeguard exams and enclose copies of my certificates.

In the future, I hope to study leisure management and business. I would be very grateful for the experience I would gain from this position.

I am available for interview immediately and able to start work on 1st June. I look forward to hearing from you.

Concluding signature

Yours sincerely,

Pat O'Connor

Remember ...

○ In your opening, if you do not know the person's name, write 'Dear Sir/Madam,'.

○ When signing off, use 'Yours sincerely,' if you know the person's name, and 'Yours faithfully,' if you don't. Don't forget to use a capital 'Y' for 'Yours'!

○ Watch out for errors in punctuation when writing addresses. Look closely at the example opposite.

○ This is a serious letter, so avoid slang, misspellings or inappropriate humour.

WHY DON'T YOU...

Write a letter of application for a job to one of the following people:

● The manager of the local cinema

● The owner of a restaurant

● The director of a summer camp

● The owner of a sports shop

● The head of MTV ®

Letter of Complaint

Now look at this formal letter of complaint.

52 Brook Lawn,
Walkinstown,
Dublin 12.

28th January 2011

Mr M. Sullivan,
Manager,
Pete's Eats,
Walkinstown,
Dublin 12.

Dear Mr Sullivan,

      I am writing to inform you of my dissatisfaction with your restaurant. My friends and I ordered a pizza there last Friday and were very disappointed with the quality of the food and the attitude of the staff.

      The pizza was not properly heated and had cold spots in the middle. The toppings were not those that we had ordered. When we pointed this out to our waiter, he was rude and accused us of having made a mistake. The cutlery on the table was dirty and the standard of hygiene in the bathrooms was appalling.

      In my opinion, your food is overpriced and your restaurant is a health hazard. For these reasons I will be reporting you to the Food Safety Authority and I will not be recommending your establishment to anyone.

Yours sincerely,
David O'Donoghue

Write a letter of complaint to one of the following:

- The owner of a local bowling alley about the dirty equipment.

- A fast-food outlet where you found a hair in your chips.

- A swimming pool with no lifeguard.

- A mobile phone shop with faulty goods.

- An outdoor pursuits centre with terrible food.

Letter of Enquiry

Here is a formal letter of enquiry.

'The Lodge',
Garretstown,
Bantry,
Co. Cork.

12th September 2011

Environmental Protection Agency,
11 Kildare Street,
Dublin 2.

Dear Sir/Madam,

I am writing to you on behalf of the first-year C.S.P.E. class in St Mary's Secondary School, Bantry. I wish to enquire about setting up a recycling scheme in our school.

As part of our C.S.P.E. course we need to complete a project to improve the environment in the area. Our teacher told us that we should contact your agency for more information. I would be grateful if you would forward any material about similar projects in other schools. In particular, we are interested in finding out about recycling cans and bottles. I enclose a stamped addressed envelope so that you can reply quickly.

I look forward to hearing from you on this matter in the near future. Thank you very much for your assistance.

Yours faithfully,
Pauline McCarthy

Write a letter of enquiry to one of the following people:

- Your favourite singer, asking for information about his or her fan club.

- The Spanish embassy, asking for information about Spain for a school project.

- Your local T.D., asking if he or she would be willing to visit your class to discuss youth issues.

- The director of a summer course, looking for more information and prices.

- The owner of a hotel, asking if they have found an item you lost.

Reports

Most reports have **four** sections.

- **Introduction:** Briefly outline the situation or problem and state the purpose of the report.

- **Information:** Step-by-step, give the facts in detail, perhaps using statistics or examples.

- **Conclusion:** Summarise the main points and explain why certain elements were successful or unsuccessful.

- **Recommendations:** Suggest solutions for future problems, these must be realistic and practical.

Always bear in mind who will be reading the report!

> A report is an account of a problem or situation. It must be factual and clear.

Write a report for the town council on a local fundraising project with which you were involved.

Before writing, plan your report using the four headings below:

1. Introduction
- Chernobyl Children's Project
- Filling container truck
- Dry goods/toys/clothes/blankets

Report on Local Fundraising Project

3. Conclusion
- Generosity of most people
- Volume of material received
- But junk and rubbish also donated
- Not enough publicity
- Hours too long for volunteers

2. Information
- Location of container — MacCarthy's Supermarket car park
- Duration — two weeks
- Drop-off times: 10 am–10 pm
- Volunteers for drop-off times, sorting goods, publicity
- Details of goods received
- Busy times — morning and evenings — other times quiet

4. Recommendations:
- Junk and rubbish should be refused
- More publicity
- Limited opening times

Report on Local Fundraising Project

Introduction
The Chernobyl Children's Project asked the community to get
involved in fundraising for the orphans in Belarus. The
community decided to fill a container truck with goods to
be transported to Belarus. Donations of clothes, dry goods,
blankets, medical supplies and toys were requested.

Information
A container truck was parked in the car park of MacCarthy's
Supermarket for the duration of the project. Over the course
of two weeks, people were encouraged to drop off goods between
10 am and 10 pm. A rota of volunteers was set up in order
to receive, sort and pack the goods. Other volunteers put
up posters to raise awareness of the project. An enormous
volume of goods was received, mostly of very high quality.
Many people bought goods in the supermarket for donation. The
busiest drop-off times were early in the morning, lunchtime
and early in the evening. Other times were very quiet.

Conclusion
From observation of the project, the generosity of many people
is clear. However, a minority of people took the opportunity
to clean out their attics, and contributed worthless and
broken items. It was felt that there was not enough publicity,
and that the posters were unclear, particularly about drop-off
times. It was difficult to find enough volunteers to man the
container truck for the full day.

Recommendations
Due to these conclusions, it is recommended that, in future,
the following steps be taken for a project of this type:

1) Material should be quickly examined on arrival, and
   inappropriate goods should be refused.

2) Publicity must be given more attention. Local
   newsletters and radio stations should be asked to get
   involved.

3) Drop-off times should be limited to the busiest times.
   Finding volunteers would not then be a problem.

Write about one of the following:

- Some pupils have been misbehaving on the school bus. The bus company has complained to the school. All pupils who travel on the bus have been asked to submit a report to the principal.

- You have witnessed a serious traffic accident. Write a report for the Gardaí.

- Your family have returned from a disastrous holiday abroad. Write a report for the travel company to help their investigation.

- Write a report on the condition of your school gym to explain to the Department of Education and Science why a new building is necessary.

- You are submitting a report to the Gaisce Awards Committee explaining what you have done to deserve your bronze medal. You have to describe an adventurous activity, a new skill or involvement in community affairs.

Dabble in Drama!

In this chapter you will read extracts from many different plays to learn about:

- Opening scenes
- Character
- Conflict
- Humour
- Staging and setting
- Closing scenes

And you will:

- Try some acting yourself!

Over the next few pages you will read extracts from various plays but this is not 'real' drama.
If you read the script from your favourite TV programme it would not be the same as watching it. When you go to a play you see and hear things, you do not read. So remember, while you are reading the page, you should be trying to see a stage.

OPENING SCENE

The **opening** scene of a play, a TV programme or a film has to catch the audience's attention or else we won't keep watching. In the following scene, the writer introduces us to important characters and makes us wonder what is going to happen next.

A First Confession

Scene One adapted from the short story
by Frank O'Connor

Scene 1 A kitchen in Cork City (1950s)

Granny comes into the kitchen. She is wearing a black shawl and carrying a pair of boots in her hands. She is also wearing a long black dress. Her hair is in a bun. When she comes on stage she is singing 'The Banks of My Own Lovely Lee', or something similar. She puts the boots down by the fire.

Granny: There now, that should keep them warm for me. Sure the Bishop of Cork himself wouldn't have as good a fire. *(She fixes the fire.)* Be the Lord God, all of this hard work would put a great thirst on you. *(She straightens up.)* Maybe there's a dropeen of porter left in the press. I'll go and see. *(She walks over to the press at the other side of the stage, takes a jug of porter and a glass, drinks and wipes her mouth with the back of her hand.)* Oh, the devil is in it. *(Pause)* Sure what's the harm. You're only auld once. *(She puts the porter back in the press.)* Maybe now I could have a bite to eat. That's if I could have a go at cooking the spuds and sausages. *(She goes to the door of the kitchen and calls out.)* Nora, Nora, have you eara notion where the sausages are for the dinner? *(Nora is upstairs.)*

Nora: I left them in the press for you, Granny.

Granny: Right so. I'll get them and put them on to cook. Let you come down here to help me.

Nora: I'll be down in a minute, Granny.

(Granny starts to sing again. She takes the sausages out of the press. She puts these into a saucepan. She takes some potatoes out of a bag, and puts these, without washing them, in on top of the sausages. She pours water on the lot.)

Granny: Be the holy now, there's a meal fit for a king. *(She goes over and puts the saucepan on the fire. She takes the boots from the hob and puts them on the kitchen table.)* They should be warm enough by now. Maybe I'll have another sup of porter. *(She goes to the press. Nora comes into the room. She has pigtails and is fat. She is wearing a uniform. As soon as Granny sees Nora she pushes away the porter in a hurry, so that the girl doesn't notice.)*

Granny: Nora, that wasn't long you spent upstairs. I thought you were supposed to change your uniform.

Nora: Sure there's no rush. I'll change it later.

Granny: You'd better. Before your Mammy comes home.

Nora: What's for dinner? *(She smells the air suspiciously.)*

Granny: Spuds and sausages. *(Nora goes to the fire to see. She lifts the pot lid and holds her nose. Granny wipes her mouth to hide the evidence.)* Is there any sign of that brother of yours?

Nora: I have no idea where he is. He was supposed to come home with me. He must have got kept back as usual. The little caffler. He has his last Communion class with Mrs Walsh this afternoon too. He's making his first confession tomorrow.

Granny: First confession how are ya! That fellow has so many sins on his soul, he wouldn't know how to confess them. *(Noise at door)* That's probably him at the door now. *(The door opens and Jackie comes in. He is small. His hair is cut very short. He is wearing short trousers. He is younger than Nora. He puts his schoolbag on the table. Granny lays the table.)*

Nora: Well, what kept ya? *(Jackie pretends he doesn't hear. He puts his tongue out at her behind her back and helps Granny lay the table. He takes the boots off but Granny puts them back in the centre of the table again.)* I said where were you? You're very late. Granny has your dinner ready.

Jackie: It's none of your business.

Nora: Granny, did you hear that?

Granny: Sure he doesn't mean it, the wee chap. Sit down here and have yer dinner. *(She brings the saucepan over to the table. They reluctantly sit down. Granny puts her dinner out and brings it over to the fire. She puts the plate on the hob.)* Salt. Why did I forget the salt? It must be old age. *(She goes to the press and pours herself out a glass of porter. Nora gets up and puts her dinner in a bucket while this is happening.)*

Jackie: Granny!

Granny: *(Still at the press, her back turned.)* What is it now?

Jackie: Nora's after throwing her dinner away.

Nora: Liar!

Granny: Are you two ever goin' to stop fighting? *(She turns to the table.)* **Well, isn't she a marvellous girl. Nora, you've finished your dinner entirely. That deserves a penny. And what about Jackie?**

Jackie: If she doesn't eat hers, I'm not eating mine. *(He stands up to put the dinner in the bucket. Nora grabs him and pushes him back down.)*

Nora: I'll make him eat it, Granny. The dirty little caffler. Here, give me that. *(She grabs the spoon out of his hand and tries to force-feed him. Jackie struggles. In the process the dinner gets thrown over Granny's boots.)*

Granny: *(Takes up the boots and starts to clean them off with her apron.)* **Now look at what you did, wicked boy. That's the last dinner I'll ever cook for you. Ruined my good boots that I haven't even worn this past year or more to keep them new. Wait 'til your mother comes home and you'll hear more about this. Where's me stick until I hit him a belt.**

Nora: Go on Granny, get him. He deserves it. I'll hold him for you. *(She tries to grab Jackie. He lifts up a breadknife from the table.)*

Jackie: Keep away! Keep away from me the pair of ye. If ya come near me again I'll stick this in ya. *(He gets under the table.)* **Now, see if you can get me.**

Granny: Mother of God, he's a murderer!

Nora: Granny, I'm all sore from Jackie. Me legs are paining all over. Look at him now. I'll have to get out of here before he kills me. *(pause)* Can I go down to the post-office to get your pension?

Granny: This is a terrible state of affairs. That boy will turn into a bad lot if he's not careful. *(She goes to the press and takes out a pension book. She also takes out the empty jug of porter.)* **Here girl. Do as you said and run and get my pension for me. Take a shilling for yourself for sweets. You deserve it. Go quickly now before he strikes at you. I'm not staying with him another minute!** *(She shakes her fist at him.)* **This is not the last you'll hear of what has happened young man, if I have any say in it. I'll be back later to deal with you.** *(They both exit. Nora gesticulates silently at Jackie before she leaves.)*

Jackie: *(Coming out from under the table.)* **That sister of mine would turn anyone into a murderer. If Granny wasn't living here in the first place none of this would have happened. I'm done for anyway. I can't stop committing sins and tomorrow I have to make my first confession. What I need is some advice.** *(pause)* **Oh – I nearly forgot. Mrs Walsh will be waiting to give her last First Communion class.** *(He grabs his bag and exits.)*

DIVE IN!

1. What is Granny doing at the start of the scene?

2. What is Granny going to make for dinner?

3. What does Nora say about her brother's first confession?

4. How do you know that Jackie doesn't like Nora?

5. What does Granny send Nora to get for her?

TAKE THE PLUNGE!

6. Name the three characters who were introduced in this scene. Choose one and say what you learned about them. Ⓟ Ⓠ Ⓔ

7. What do you think is going to happen next?

8. What other questions come into your head about the people in this play?

9. What sort of play do you think this is going to be (sad, happy, scary, funny, adventurous …)? Give reasons for your answer. Ⓟ Ⓠ Ⓔ *at least 2 reasons*

10. Did you think this was a good opening scene? Ⓟ Ⓠ Ⓔ

WHY DON'T YOU…

Think about how opening Ⓡ scenes introduce us to people. Split into pairs and prepare a scene where two people meet and shake hands. Choose situations from the list below. You must decide why these people are meeting and how they will shake hands.

- Prisoner and lawyer
- Batman and the Joker
- Politician and person in street
- Two old friends reunited
- Principal and parent
- Two soldiers from opposite sides
- TV presenter and guest
- Two footballers on different teams
- Beauty and the Beast
- A human and an alien

OR

When we meet people in Ireland we shake hands, in France they kiss cheeks, Eskimos rub noses and the Japanese bow. In pairs, try to invent a new form of greeting.

OR

Think about how a character's actions can tell us as much about them as what they say. Fold a page from your copybook and imagine it is a letter you have just received. For the class, mime your reaction as you read the letter. The class must guess the contents of the letter from your expressions and gestures.

THRASH IT OUT!

Do you think Jackie and Nora are a typical brother and sister? Discuss your opinion in class.

CHARACTERS

The audience gets to know the characters in a play by **listening** to what they say, **watching** what they do and **hearing** what other characters say about them.

Blood Brothers

Willy Russell

Edward and Mickey are twins who were separated at birth because their mother was too poor to keep both of them. Edward was adopted by a well-off family; Mickey stayed with his mother. Neither knows of the other's existence. Here they meet for the first time by chance.

Bored and petulant, Mickey aged seven sits and shoots an imaginary Sammy (his older brother). Edward, also aged seven, appears. He is bright and forthcoming.

Edward:	Hello.
Mickey:	*(suspiciously)* Hello.
Edward:	I've seen you before.
Mickey:	Where?
Edward:	You were playing with some boys near my house.
Mickey:	Do you live up in the park?

*petulant –
sulky*

Edward:	Yes. Are you going to come and play up there again?
Mickey:	No. I would do but I'm not allowed.
Edward:	Why?
Mickey:	'Cos me mam says.
Edward:	Well, my mammy doesn't allow me to play down here actually.
Mickey:	'Gis a sweet.
Edward:	All right. *(He offers a bag from his pocket.)*
Mickey:	*(shocked)* What?
Edward:	Here.
Mickey:	*(Trying to work out the catch. Suspiciously taking one.)* Can I have another one. For our Sammy?
Edward:	Yes, of course. Take as many as you want.
Mickey:	*(Taking a handful.)* Are you soft?
Edward:	I don't think so.
Mickey:	Round here if y' ask for a sweet, y' have to ask about twenty million times. An' y' know what?
Edward:	*(Sitting beside Mickey.)* What?
Mickey:	They still don't bleedin' give y' one. Sometimes our Sammy does but y' have to be dead careful if our Sammy gives y' a sweet.
Edward:	Why?
Mickey:	Cos, if our Sammy gives y' a sweet he's usually weed on it first.
Edward:	*(Exploding in giggles.)* Oh, that sounds like super fun.
Mickey:	It is. If y' our Sammy.
Edward:	Do you want to come and play?
Mickey:	I might do. But I'm not playin' now cos I'm pissed off.
Edward:	*(awed)* Pissed off. You say smashing things don't you? Do you know any more words like that?
Mickey:	Yeh. Yeh, I know loads of words like that. Y' know, like the 'F' word.
Edward:	*(clueless)* Pardon?
Mickey:	The 'F' word. *(Edward is still puzzled. Mickey looks round to check that he cannot be overheard, then whispers the word to Edward. The two of them immediately wriggle and giggle with glee.)*
Edward:	What does it mean?
Mickey:	I don't know. But it sounds good though, doesn't it?
Edward:	Fantastic. When I get home I'll look it up in the dictionary.
Mickey:	In the what?
Edward:	The dictionary. Don't you know what a dictionary is?
Mickey:	'Course I do … It's a, it's a thingy innit?
Edward:	A book which explains the meaning of words …
Mickey:	The meaning of words, yeh. Our Sammy'll be here soon. I hope he's in a good mood. He's dead mean sometimes.
Edward:	Why?
Mickey:	It's cos he's got a plate in his head.
Edward:	A plate. In his head?

Mickey: Yeh. When he was little, me mam was at work an' our Donna Marie was supposed to be lookin' after him but he fell out the window an' broke his head. So they took him to the hospital an' put a plate in his head.

Edward: A plate. A dinner plate?

Mickey: I don't think so, cos our Sammy's head's not really that big. I think it must have been one of them little plates that you have bread off.

Edward: A side plate?

Mickey: No, it's on the top.

Edward: And ... and can you see the shape of it, in his head.

Mickey: I suppose, I suppose if y' looked under his hair.

Edward: *(After a reflective pause.)* You know the most smashing things. Will you be my best friend?

Mickey: Yeh. If y' want.

Edward: What's your name?

Mickey: Michael Johnstone. But everyone calls me Mickey. What's yours?

Edward: Edward Lyons.

Mickey: D' they call y' Eddie?

Edward: No.

Mickey: Well, I will.

Edward: Will you?

Mickey: Yeh. How old are y' Eddie?

Edward: Seven.

Mickey: I'm older than you. I'm nearly eight.

Edward: Well, I'm nearly eight, really.

Mickey: What's your birthday?

Edward: July the eighteenth.

Mickey: So is mine.

Edward: Is it really?

Mickey: Eh, we were born on the same day ... that means we can be blood brothers. Do you wanna be my blood brother, Eddie?

Edward: Yes, please. *(Producing a penknife.)*

Mickey: It hurts y' know. *(He puts a nick in his hand.)* Now, give us yours. *(Mickey nicks Edward's hand, then they clamp hands together.)* See this means we are blood brothers, an' that we always have to stand by each other. Now you say after me: 'I will always defend my brother'.

Edward: I will always defend my brother ...

Mickey: And stand by him.

Edward: And stand by him.

Mickey: And share all my sweets with him.

Edward: And share ... *(Sammy leaps in front of them, gun in hand, pointed at them.)*

1. Why have Mickey and Edward not met before?

2. Mickey is shocked when Edward gives him a sweet. Why?

3. How do we know Mickey is more 'streetwise' than Edward?

4. Do you think Edward has had more schooling than Mickey? Give a reason for your answer.

5. Why is Mickey afraid of Sammy?

6. From the list below, choose three words that you think best describe Mickey:

   defensive, suspicious, rude, angry, tough, friendly, lonely, innocent

   Taking these words one at a time, find evidence in the text to support your description. **PQE**

7. From the list below, choose three words that you think best describe Edward:

   friendly, open, generous, loving, lonely, innocent, curious, enthusiastic

   Taking these words one at a time, find evidence in the text to support your description. **PQE**

8. How can you tell that the two boys are from very different backgrounds? Explain your answer fully. **PQE**

9. The boys speak very differently. Pick out some examples which show this. **PQE**

10. How did the ending of this extract make you feel?

Read this extract aloud with the person next to you. Decide who will be Mickey and who will be Edward. Do your best to act and sound like the character you are portraying.

OR

Divide into pairs and sit facing each other. Decide who will be the leader and who will be the follower. The follower must copy the movements of the leader exactly. You are pretending that you are facing a mirror. Try to mime some everyday activities like shaving, combing your hair, brushing your teeth, washing your face, putting on make-up, etc.

OR

Create your own character in your copybook, using the following headings:

- Name
- Age
- Three physical characteristics *(how they look)*
- Voice
- Personality traits *(what sort of person they are)*
- Background *(where they live, job, family, etc.)*
- Likes/dislikes

Here are some suggestions to help you get started:

- A bold child
- Mad Tom
- A young priest
- A new pupil
- A successful business person
- A comedian
- A member of a boy/girl band
- A TV chef
- An athlete
- A hairdresser

Divide into pairs and pretend you are the character that you created in the previous exercise. Introduce yourself to the other person and have a chat in character. For homework, write out the conversation that you had.

CONFLICT

Conflict occurs when people disagree with each other. When there is conflict on stage, the audience does not know what is going to happen next and this keeps their attention. This is called **tension** or **suspense**.

The Field

John B. Keane

The Bull McCabe and his son Tadhg have been renting a field from a widow named Maggie Butler. She has decided to sell the field and they are determined to buy it. On the day of the auction a stranger named William Dee appears and begins to bid against the Bull.

Mick: I have £200. Do I have any advance on £200? On £200? I have £200 from Mr Thady McCabe of Inchabawn … *(Again William is the subject of all eyes.)* Is this to be the final bid? There is a reserve and I will negotiate by private treaty with the highest bidder. C'mon now, ladies and gentlemen. Before I close this public auction, do I hear any advance on £200?

William: *(casually)* Guineas!

Mick: Any advance on £200?

William: Two hundred guineas.

Tadhg: What's guineas?

Bull: He should be disqualified. There's no such thing as a guinea going these days.

William: All right. I'll bid £300.

(An audible hush.)

Mick: *(nervously)* I have £300 … have I any advance on £300? I'm bid £300. Do I hear £350? Do I hear £350? No! … In that event, I'll call a recess for a day and negotiate by private treaty.

(Mick is about to turn away but William rises and stops him.)

William: What time do you propose to start tomorrow?

Mick: Oh, some time in the morning. We can't all be on the dot like you. These people here are hardworking people with little time to spare.

William: What guarantee have I that you won't close the deal with him? *(Indicating Bull.)*

Mick: Now, let that be the least of your worries. Everything is nice and legal here.

William: I take it then that my bid being the highest, you'll give me something in writing until morning.

Mick: *(anger)* You'll get no bloody writing from me … You'll be here in the morning if you want to bid again.

William:	Bid against whom?
Mick:	*(For the benefit of Maggie Butler.)* You'll bid until this woman's reserve has been reached. There's no one going to wrong an old woman, not while I'm on my feet, Mister. I'll give you a guarantee of that.
William:	How much is the reserve?
Mick:	£800.
William:	That's not beyond me and I'm prepared to bid again. When can I see the field? *(Tadhg and Bull step forward.)*
Tadhg:	Stay away from that field.
Bull:	There's cattle of ours there.
William:	If the field is for auction, I'm entitled to have a look at it.
Bull:	Use your head while you're able. Stay away!
Tadhg:	That's right! Get the hell out of here now … while you can.
Maggie:	You can see my field any time, sir.
Bull:	*(roars)* Shut up, you oul' fool! What about my claim?
Maggie:	You've no claim!
Bull:	*(dangerously)* Look out for yourself, you! Look out for yourself. *(He cows the old woman.)*
William:	I'll be back when you open in the morning.
Bull:	That field is mine! Remember that! I'll pay a fair price. God Almighty! 'Tis a sin to cover grass and clover with concrete. *(Maggie Butler rises and moves towards the doorway.)*
Maggie:	*(to Maimie)* I'll have to be goin'. There's no one in the house but myself.
Bull:	You should remember that! *(Maggie looks back startled. William acknowledges Maggie's exit.)*
Bull:	*(to William)* Get out while you're clean!
William:	I'll be back in the morning … and this time I'll be with my solicitor. *(William exiting.)*
Bull:	You might be back with more than your solicitor.
	(William exits. Bull, Tadhg and Mick go into a huddle at the counter. The lights fade.)

DIVE IN!

1. Where do you first notice tension in this scene?

2. Who seems to be the most nervous character?

3. Why do you think William wants 'something in writing until morning'?

4. At what point does the tension increase? Explain your answer.

5. What do you think the Bull means when he says, 'You might be back with more than your solicitor'?

TAKE THE PLUNGE!

6. In the stage directions, the writer is telling the actors how to say their lines. Reread the extract and pick out two examples where you feel the stage directions are very important. **PQE**

7. What tells you that the Bull McCabe and his son may be violent men? Explain your answer fully. **PQE**

8. What do you think of the way the Bull speaks to Maggie?

9. Which character do you feel the most sympathy for and why? **PQE**

10. Did this extract hold your attention? Would you be curious to see how the play ends? What do you think will happen?

WHY DON'T YOU...

Draw a rectangle in your copybook to represent the stage. Decide who is the most powerful character in this scene. Decide where you would place him or her in relation to all the other characters in order to make this point. **R**

OR

Divide into groups and act out a scene based on one of the following scenarios. You can introduce extra characters if you like.

- Your mother takes you shopping. You have disagreements over what is suitable attire!

- You go shopping with a friend. They try on something you really like. You need to persuade them not to buy it yet manage to buy it yourself.

- You are sitting on the couch with members of your family. There is a disagreement about what will be watched on TV.

- You are a teacher at a parent/teacher meeting and you have a very bold pupil in your class. When the mother arrives, you realise she believes her child is an angel. How do you tell her the truth? How does she react?

- You are going out with someone of a different race and your parents see you with them. They do not approve. You think they are racist. A heated conversation follows.

HUMOUR

HUMOUR

Read this extract. Do you think it's funny?

Skungpoomery

Ken Campbell

Nicholas Wibble is a policeman. In this extract his mother is helping him to get ready to go to work.

PC Nicholas Wibble:	But all the other policemen wear boots.
Mrs Wibble:	That's because they haven't got nice sandals.
Wibble:	Well why've I always got to be different?
Mrs Wibble:	It's not a case of 'being different', Nicholas, it's a case of being sensible. It's unhealthy to have your feet laced up inside those big clumping boots all day in the hot weather –
Wibble:	O Mum.
Mrs Wibble:	I don't want to hear any more about it, Nicholas.
Wibble:	Anyway these sandals pinch my feet, Mum.
Mrs Wibble:	Nicholas! You little fibber! We got those sandals at Clarks and we both looked down at the X-Ray machine together and we both saw that you had plenty of room in those sandals. Nicholas!
Wibble:	Wh-at?
Mrs Wibble:	What's that?
Wibble:	What's what?
Mrs Wibble:	On your tie?
Wibble:	Nothing.
Mrs Wibble:	Egg dribblings. Look at that. And I all nicely ironed it yesterday morning and now you've dribbled your egg on it. Come here. *(She leads him by his tie to the bowl and cloth.)*
Wibble:	O Mum.
Mrs Wibble:	O and it's not coming out look. It'll have to be put in to soak.
Wibble:	Oh no, Mum – look I'm due on the beat in five minutes. I can't wait while you soak it.
Mrs Wibble:	Well I am certainly not letting you go out with your tie in that state.
Wibble:	The Sergeant gets really cross if I'm late.
Mrs Wibble:	Well you'll just have to wear your bow tie.

Wibble:	O no.
Mrs Wibble:	Nicholas!
Wibble:	O look all the other policemen wear ordinary straight ties.
Mrs Wibble:	Come here and let's put it on you and have less of your nonsense. Your Aunty Glad gave you this nice bow tie – and did you write her a proper thank you letter?
Wibble:	Yes.
Mrs Wibble:	Good boy. *(Looking at his face.)* Hanky? *(He supplies it.)* Lick. *(He licks it and she wipes a bit of dirt off his face with it.)*
Wibble:	'Bye then, Mum.
Mrs Wibble:	Kiss please. I've done you some sandwiches.
Wibble:	O Mum, can't I eat in the canteen with the other policemen?
Mrs Wibble:	O you make me so cross, Nicholas. We've just managed to get rid of all your spots and now you want to go into that nasty canteen and eat greasy fried stuff.
Wibble:	It's not all greasy fried stuff in there, Mum.
Mrs Wibble:	You're an ungrateful boy, Nicholas.
Wibble:	O I'm not ungrateful at all, Mum. I'm grateful. I really am. It's all right. I'll take the sandwiches. And I'll enjoy them.
Mrs. Wibble:	I should think so. O Nicholas! I ironed those trousers at the weekend and now look at them. They're all baggy at the knees. Don't you hitch then up when you sit down?
Wibble:	Yes.
Mrs Wibble:	Take them off and let me give them a quick press.
Wibble:	O no, Mum – look I'm going to be ever so late now.
Mrs Wibble:	Take them off, Nicholas, it won't take a moment.
Wibble:	No.
Mrs Wibble:	Nicholas!!!
Wibble:	Ooooooooooooh! *(Mrs Wibble waits. He sulkily removes his trousers revealing 'Chilprufe' underpants. Mrs Wibble takes the trousers off and returns with an iron and ironing board.)*
Mrs Wibble:	Right.
Wibble:	Please hurry up, Mum.
Mrs Wibble:	I'm being as quick as I can, Nicholas. *(She is now ironing.)* The number of times I've been on to you, Nicholas, to just think before you go to bed at night, what you're going to need in the morning, and go over it and check it's all right then; there's absolutely no need for this breakfast time misery. But you, you never seem to know what you're at or what you're doing. *(The phone rings. She answers the iron holding it next to her ear.)* Hello? Hello? Yahhhhhhhhhhhhhhhhhh! *(In her agony, she puts the iron down on the trousers.)* Butter! Get the butter, Nicholas.
Wibble:	Oh yes, here you are. *(He shoves a full round soft marge pack onto his Mum's ear. They tie the pack to her ear with a scarf.)*
Mrs Wibble:	Nicholas, you will be the death of me.
Wibble:	How's it my fault Mum? If you stick the iron in your ear?
Mrs Wibble:	Nicholas, just shut up! *(Clouts him.)* Ooooof. *(The pain of the burn.)* Go and answer it.

Wibble:	*(Picking up the phone.)* That's all right. That's not so good. That's very good. That's just first class. That's awful. That's good. That's rotten.
Mrs Wibble:	Who is it?
Wibble:	It's Auntie Glad. She just wanted some help sorting her tomatoes. O no! O Mum look what you've done now! *(He picks up the trousers revealing a huge burn hole.)* O no.
Mrs Wibble:	I'm not the least bit sympathetic, Nicholas. It's just a direct result of your own thoughtlessness.
Wibble:	What am I going to do now?
Mrs Wibble:	Well you'll just have to wear your shorts.
Wibble:	O no!
Mrs Wibble:	They're in the airing cupboard.
Wibble:	I can't wear short trousers on the beat, Mum!
Mrs Wibble:	Of course you can. It's a nice warm morning. Go and get them before I get very cross indeed. I don't know how I am going to mend these. They'll need the most enormous patch. O come along. Let's get you out of the house. *(She goes off and returns immediately with the shorts.)* Get into those and off you go. Then I can have a cup of tea in peace.
Wibble:	*(Miserably and slowly dons his shorts.)* This is going to be the worst day of my life. *(Goes.)*
Mrs Wibble:	And he's forgotten his sandwiches. *(She walks off.)*

DIVE IN!

1. What sort of person do you think Mrs Wibble is?

2. What age does Mrs Wibble seem to think Nicholas is?

3. In your opinion, what is the funniest moment in this scene?

TAKE THE PLUNGE!

4. Some of the things the characters say are very humorous. Choose three examples. **P Q E**

5. Pick a moment of slapstick comedy from this extract.

WHY DON'T YOU...

In pairs, act out this scene for the class.

OR

Draw a picture of poor PC Wibble when he finally gets to work.

OR

Write an essay beginning with the sentence, 'It was the worst day of my life …' **R**

THRASH IT OUT!

All children need something to ignore, And that's what parents were created for.

Ogden Nash

In groups, talk about a time when your parents completely embarrassed you or a moment when you completely embarrassed your parents.

When the humour in a situation comes from people hurting themselves, it is called slapstick comedy. The most common example of this is in cartoons like *Tom and Jerry* or *The Itchy and Scratchy Show* on *The Simpsons!*

Father Ted

Graham Linehan and Arthur Mathews

Just like a play on the stage, a programme on television also needs a script. This is called the screenplay. Look at the example below.

Father Ted and Father Dougal have spent all night trying to compose a song to enter in the Eurosong Contest. They are playing it for the first time to Father Jack and Mrs Doyle.

Scene 3
Set: PAROCHIAL HOUSE
Ted is sitting on a stool with his guitar. Dougal stands beside him, behind the keyboard. An expectant Mrs Doyle and a grumpy Father Jack are are on the sofa, watching them. Dougal presses one button and a drumbeat starts. He then stands back, not touching the keyboard for the rest of the song. Ted starts playing his guitar -- the same note for each line.

Ted: 'My lovely horse,
Running through the fields
Where are you going
With your fetlocks blowing in the wind.'
Shot of Jack and Mrs Doyle taking this in.

Dougal and Ted: *(chorus)*
'I want to shower you with sugar-lumps
And ride you over fences
Polish your hooves every day
And bring you to the horse dentist.
My lovely horse
You're a pony no more
Running around with a man on your
back, like a train in the night.'
Ted does the one note again, and then moves his hand up the fretboard to do the final note. It goes wrong.

Ted: Oh, wait, wait ...
He tries again. It sounds off.

Ted: Wait, I can do this.
He tries again. This time it sounds reasonably ok. The song ends. Ted puts the guitar upright and leans on it. Pause.

Ted: It needs a bit of work here and there, but what do you think in general?

198

Ted: *Ted and Dougal look expectantly at Jack and Mrs Doyle. Mrs Doyle cannot conceal her look of distaste. Jack looks at her, looks at them, picks up a shotgun and shoots the guitar. (looks at shattered guitar)* : Right ....

SCENE 4
SET: PAROCHIAL HOUSE
Ted and Dougal are sitting on the sofa, looking glum.

Ted: Father Jack's right. It's a terrible song. It really is. God almighty, what were we thinking?

Dougal: Ah, it's not that bad, Ted.

Ted: Well, the lyrics are fine. There's no problem there. But there's no tune. It's just one note over and over again. Oh, God … and I went and booked time in that studio. I hope we can cancel.

Dougal: Ted. Can I put on my favourite Eurosong? Maybe that'll cheer us up.

Ted: Yes. That might help. What is it?

Dougal goes to the stereo and puts on his record.

Dougal: Nin Huugen and the Huugen Notes. It came fifth in the 'Song for Norway' competition in 1976.

Ted: Where on earth did you get that?

Dougal: Ah, you know me, Ted. I've always had an interest in rare, hard-to-find records.

Ted: Dougal, can I remind you again, you've only got one record. That's not really an 'interest'. Maybe if you developed an interest in records that weren't hard to find, you might actually be able to find some records.

Dougal has put the record on, and it's actually quite tuneful.

Ted: That's not too bad, actually.

Dougal: Oh, actually, that's the B side. I'll turn it over.

Ted: No, leave it, leave it …

Dougal: It's nice enough, isn't it?

Ted: Yes. If only we'd come up with something like that.

Pause. A strange sly look comes over Ted's face.

Ted: I suppose not many people would have heard that song.

Dougal: Suppose not. First time I've heard it anyway.

Ted: A lot of people wouldn't really have much of an interest in the B side of a song that came fifth in 'A Song for Norway'. What are the band doing now?

Dougal: Oh, God, Ted, it's a terrible story. They all died in a plane crash along with all the people who were involved in the song – the producer, the studio engineer, their manager …

Ted: … the people who owned the publishing rights?

Dougal: Oh, yes.

Ted: Tsk, that's terrible. *(Pause)* Eh, Dougal …?

Dougal: Yeah?

Ted: Wouldn't it be nice to commemorate all those talented people by keeping their music alive?

Dougal: What?

Ted: Say, if we borrowed that tune for 'My Lovely Horse'. It'd help us out and commemorate their memory at the same time.

Dougal: So we wouldn't just be stealing the tune?

Ted: Dougal, there's no way, just because we take their tune and put our lyrics over it, that we're stealing the tune.

Dougal: No?

Ted: No. You'd have to be mad to jump to that conclusion. What we're doing is celebrating their memory. Secretly. Don't tell anyone, incidentally.

Dougal: Right. And I suppose, if the song wins and we make money out of it, we could give it to their relatives.

Pause

Ted: … Yyyyyyyeah … we'll play it by ear.

1. Is Father Ted good at playing the guitar?

2. How do you know that Father Jack doesn't like the song?

3. What is Father Dougal's favourite Eurosong and where did it come from?

4. What is Father Ted's idea to improve their song?

5. What did you think of the lyrics of 'My Lovely Horse'?

6. Why are the directions in the screenplay so important? **P Q E**

7. What argument does Ted use to persuade Dougal that it's okay to use the Norwegian song? **P Q E**

8. How do you know that Dougal is less intelligent than Ted?

Draw a storyboard ® for this scene. Your drawings don't need to be good, but they need to illustrate:

● What the camera is looking at in each shot.

● Whether the camera is in close-up or far away from the action.

● The movement of the actors.

OR

See if you can find a copy of this episode of *Father Ted* and watch it. Try to list five reasons why it is funnier to watch this scene than it is to read it.

OR

In groups of four, act out this scene for the class.

The Virtuous Burglar

Dario Fo

A Burglar, having forced open a window, is climbing into a third-floor apartment in a well-to-do block of flats. On one side stands a classical shaded lamp. He looks around carefully. From the dark, we see furniture, rugs, old valuable paintings emerge. The Burglar closes the shutters, then switches on the light.

Just when he is about to pull open a drawer, the telephone rings. His first panic-stricken impulse is to make off as quickly as possible but then, realising that no one in the house comes to answer it and that he has nothing to fear, he returns to where he was. He would like to ignore the ringing of the phone but cannot. He makes his way stealthily over to the phone and leaps at it. He grabs the receiver and, almost as if he wished to suffocate it, presses it against his chest, covering it with his jacket. As though to make the act seem more criminal, an increasingly feeble and suffocated sound begins to emerge from the receiver.

Burglar's Wife:	Hello. Hello. Would you kindly answer … Who's speaking?
	(The Burglar can finally let out a sigh of relief. The voice has stopped. The Burglar takes the receiver from under his jacket, raises it cautiously and puts it to his ear. Then shakes it several times and hears a kind of a groan.)
Burglar:	Oh! At last.
Burglar's Wife:	Ooooh! At last … Who's speaking?
Burglar:	*(Surprised once again.)* Maria. Is that you?
Burglar's Wife:	Yes, it's me. Why didn't you reply?
	(At this point, lit up by one of the footlights, the figure of the woman who is speaking on the phone appears on the side of the stage which has so far remained in darkness.)
Burglar:	You're crazy! Are you phoning me at work now? Suppose there had been someone in the house? You're a great help you are.
Burglar's Wife:	But you told me yourself that the owners were at their country cottage … anyway, I'm sorry, but I just couldn't stand it anymore … I was worried about you … I didn't feel well … even a few moments ago, when I was ringing up, I could hardly breathe.
Burglar:	Oh well, I'm sorry too, I didn't mean it, it never occurred to me that it might be you …
Burglar's Wife:	And just what do you mean by that?
Burglar:	Nothing, nothing … but let me get on … I've already wasted enough time.
Burglar's Wife:	Ah, I'm wasting your time now! Thank you very much. Here I am in agony, nearly sick with worry … I don't know what I am going to do with myself …

Burglar:	What are you doing?
Burglar's Wife:	I'm going through absolute hell, all because of you … and you treat me like this … charming, just charming that is … but don't worry … from now on I'm not interested … from now on don't even bother telling me where you're going, because as far as I am concerned …
Burglar:	My dear, try and be reasonable … Can't you get it into your sweet head that I am not here for fun … just this once, couldn't you let me get on with my burgling in peace?
Burglar's Wife:	There you go. You're at it again. Playing the martyr. There are plenty of people who burgle, shoplift, and even go in for armed robbery without all this fuss. Just as well you stick to petty crime, otherwise God knows what sort of state I'd be in.
Burglar:	*(Who has heard a strange noise behind him, instinctively putting his hand over the mouthpiece.)* **Quiet!** *(Fortunately it was only the sound of the grandfather clock about to strike. It strikes midnight.)*
Burglar's Wife:	What's that?
Burglar:	*(Recovering from his fright.)* It's only the grandfather clock, thank goodness.
Burglar's Wife:	What a clear sound it has! – It must be quite old. Is it very heavy?
Burglar:	*(absent-mindedly)* Might be quite … *(Suddenly realising his wife's intentions.)* Come on … You're not really expecting me to bring it home … sometimes I wonder …
Burglar's Wife:	Oh no, don't you bother your little head about me … How could you imagine that I'd ask anything like that … a nice thought from you! … You giving a little present to me! … The very idea!
Burglar:	You're mad, that's what you are … If I try to carry off that box, you tell me where to put the silverware and anything else I find.
Burglar's Wife:	In the box …
Burglar:	*(sarcastically)* You wouldn't like me to bring home a fridge? There's a nice big one through there, with a freezer department.
Burglar's Wife:	Don't raise your voice, please. You're not at home now.
Burglar:	Sorry. I got carried away.
Burglar's Wife:	Besides, you might be overheard, and you'd look singularly ill-mannered.
Burglar:	I've already said I'm sorry.
Burglar's Wife:	And anyway, I didn't say I wanted a fridge, never mind one with a freezer compartment, I wouldn't know where to put it. But I would like a little something … it's the thought that counts. I'll leave it to you. It's you that's giving the present, after all.
Burglar:	How am I supposed to know what you would like. I've got other things on my mind right now.
Burglar's Wife:	If that's all it is, I could come along and choose it myself.
Burglar:	That's all I'd need!
Burglar's Wife:	I'd love to see what a real luxury flat is like. I'd make them die with envy at the coffee morning.

Burglar: It's me that'll die from something or other, not the women at the coffee morning … I'm here to burgle this house, can you not understand that? Cheerio, see you later.

Burglar's Wife: What's the rush? Is it too much for you to be nice to me once in a while? I am your wife after all. You even married me in a church, not in a registry, so you can't get out of it.

Burglar: *(annoyed)* I've already said goodbye.

Burglar's Wife: Just a little kiss.

Burglar: Oh all right. *(He purses his lips in a comic way and emits a loud kissing sound.)*

Burglar's Wife: Do you love me?

Burglar: Yes I love you.

Burglar's Wife: Very much?

Burglar: *(At the end of his tether.)* Very, very much. But now will you put down the phone?

Burglar's Wife: You first.

Burglar: All right … me first. *(He is about to put the phone down when he hears his wife's voice assailing him loudly for the last time.)*

Burglar's Wife: Don't forget the present! *(The Burglar replaces the phone, staring at it all the while with hatred. At that moment the figure of the woman disappears in the dark. Finally alone, the Burglar begins to look around the apartment in search of his booty.)*

assailing – attacking

DIVE IN!

1. What do you think of a burglar's wife ringing him the middle of a robbery?

2. What sort of woman does the burglar's wife appear to be?

3. How do we know the burglar is nervous?

TAKE THE PLUNGE!

4. Describe the burglar's costume.

5. What type of voice do you think the wife should have? **PQE**

6. How would you light the stage?

7. What kind of house do you think this is, and how would you show this on stage? **PQE**

WHY DON'T YOU...

Put a mobile phone at the top of the room. When the teacher points at you, you must 'answer' the phone. Have a conversation with a person on the other end using only the words 'Yes' or 'No'. The class must guess what sort of news you are receiving.

OR

Pretend that you are sneaking into your house, having been out late without permission. Try to cross the classroom as slowly and quietly as possible. Give each other marks out of ten for effort.

OR

In groups, prepare an episode of *Crimeline*, detailing a 'serious' theft in your school. Try to speak like a real presenter. You might need to do a reconstruction of the theft. Here is an example.

Presenter:
Good evening.
At approximately 10.36 am on Thursday 7 April, Mary Murphy's purple fluffy pencil case disappeared from desk five, row two in classroom 3B.
A uniformed individual was sighted lurking in the vicinity.
We are appealing to this person to come forward and assist with our inquiries.
Please watch the following reconstruction.
Some scenes may be unsuitable for young children.

THRASH IT OUT!

Pretend the burglar has been apprehended. He or she is now in an interview cell with a guard. In pairs re-enact the interrogation scene.

STAGING AND SETTING

You go to 'see' and 'hear' a play, not to read it, which is why the following elements are so important:

- ☼ **Set** and **scenery** create a place on the stage.

- ☼ **Props** are any objects on stage that are moveable and that the actors use.

- ☼ **Costumes** worn by characters reveal when the play is taking place and what the characters may be like.

- ☼ **Lighting** creates atmosphere and mood, as well as highlighting important moments in the play.

- ☼ **Sound effects** and **music** also add to atmosphere and can make the play more realistic.

The Silver Sword

adapted by Stuart Henson
(from the novel by Ian Seraillier)

This extract is set during World War II in Poland. Joseph Balicki has escaped from a Nazi concentration camp. He has returned to the ruins of his family's home in Warsaw to search for his children.

The stage lights dim. One spot remains, isolating Joseph.

Joseph: I spent several more days looking for the children. One afternoon while I was poking among the rubble of my old home I found a tiny silver sword. About five inches long, it had a brass hilt engraved with a dragon breathing fire. It was a paper knife that I had once given to my wife – as a birthday present. *(He looks at the sword sadly then wipes it with care on the sleeve of his coat. He turns, suddenly aware he is being watched. Jan, who has entered silently, is squatting on the edge of the spotlight. He has his wooden 'treasure box' in one hand, in the other, a 'travelling box' with a bony grey kitten. Eyeing Joseph with suspicion, Jan turns to his box and lifts out his kitten, as if to say: 'You can't hurt us, we protect each other.' But Joseph smiles. He steps to him and strokes the kitten.)*

Joseph: *(gently)* **What's his name?**

Jan: **He hasn't got a name. He's just mine.** *(Joseph takes the kitten and holds him up admiringly. As he does so Jan slips a hand into Joseph's coat pocket and lifts a wrapped sandwich. Joseph turns back. Jan conceals the theft.)*

Joseph: **What's your name?** *(Jan pouts: turns away into the shadow; unwraps and sniffs the sandwich. After a second's thought he skips back close to Joseph.)*

Jan: Will you give me that sword?

Joseph: But it's mine.

Jan: But you found it on my pitch. This is my place.

Joseph: *(sadly)* No, this is my house – at least this rubble is what's left of it.

Jan: I'll give you food for it. *(Offers Joseph the sandwich.)*

Joseph: No thanks, I have my own. *(Hand to pocket. Pause.)* **You little thief!** *(Joseph grabs at the sandwich, but he's holding the kitten. Jan steps back and munches at it.)*

Joseph: *(conciliatory)* **Look, maybe you can help me.** *(Jan looks suspicious, but pays attention. During the next speech he takes the kitten and returns it to its box.)* **I'm searching for my family – three children. Ruth is the eldest – she'd be fifteen now. She's tall and fair.** *(He shows the photograph.)* **Then Edek, he's thirteen. And Bronia's the youngest – only five. We all lived here. I don't suppose you've seen anything of them.**

Jan: Warsaw is full of lost children. They're dirty and starving and they all look alike. *(He turns, and is almost gone when Joseph calls him back.)*

Joseph: Wait! I'll give you this sword on one condition. *(Jan comes back.)* I'm not sure that my children are dead. If you ever see Ruth or Edek or Bronia, you must tell them about our meeting. Tell them that I'm going to Switzerland to find their mother. To their grandparents' home. Tell them to follow as soon as they can. *(Pause: Jan makes no response.)* Now, listen. I'm starting off for Switzerland tonight. I don't want to walk all the way, so I'm going to jump a train. Where's the best place? *(Jan holds out his hand for the sword, takes it quickly and hides it in his 'treasure box'.)*

Jan: You will be caught and shot. Or you will freeze to death in the trucks. The nights are bitter. Your hair will be white with frost. Your fingers will turn to icicles. And when the Nazis find you, you will be stiff as the boards at the bottom of the truck. That is what happens to those who jump trains.

Joseph: You seem to know a lot about it!

Jan: I've seen it.

Joseph: Can't be helped. I must risk it. It's better than going back to the place I've come from.

Jan: I'll take you to the bend where the trains slow down. We must go the back ways – it's curfew time. If the Nazi patrols see us they'll shoot. *(Joseph struggles to keep up with Jan as he dashes from point to point in a zig-zag across the stage. Finally they rest, crouching breathless in a dim spot Right.)*

Joseph: *(After a long pause.)* I have much to thank you for and I don't even know your name. *(Another long pause: Jan says nothing.)* Have you no parents?

Jan: All I have is my cat, and this box.

Joseph: You won't come with me?

Jan: *(Ignoring the question, opening his box and examining the sword.)* This is the best of my treasures. It will bring me luck. And it will bring you luck because you gave it to me. *(Pause)* I don't usually tell people my name – it's not safe. But because you gave me the sword, I'll tell you. It's Jan.

Joseph: There are many Jans in Poland. What's your surname?

Jan: That's all. Just Jan. *(Sound of slow train approaching. Joseph stands, looks out into the darkness, back to Jan.)*

Joseph: Goodbye Jan. Remember your promise. Whatever happens, I shall not forget you. *(Blackout. The train sound builds to a climax, and fades slowly.)*

conciliatory – trying to make peace

1. What did Joseph find in the rubble?

2. What does Jan steal from Joseph?

3. There is a deal struck between Joseph and Jan. What is it?

4. Is Joseph's journey a safe one? Explain your answer.

5. Why does Jan tell Joseph his name?

6. Why do you think Joseph is in a spotlight at the beginning of the extract? **P Q E**

7. Jan stays at the edge of the spotlight. What does this tell us about his character? **P Q E**

8. If you were the director, how would you tell Jan to move on stage?

9. What sort of costumes do you think these two characters should be wearing? **P Q E**

10. Describe the music you would put with this scene. There is one sound effect you would also need. What is it?

Draw and describe the set you would design for this scene. Remember it must be portable and you have a limited budget.

OR

Make a list of the props you would need for this scene.

CLOSING SCENE

The closing scene often contains an unexpected twist or a revelation. All the aspects of the story are concluded and the audience is expected to feel some emotion like joy or sorrow. In the following scene, there is an unexpected ending.

Sive

John B. Keane

Sive is an eighteen-year-old girl who lives with her aunt and uncle, Mike and Mena Glavin, in a rural part of Ireland during the late 1950s. Her aunt Mena is a bitter and greedy woman. Mena agrees with Thomasheen, the local matchmaker, that Sive will be married to Seán Dotá. He is an old man, who is willing to pay to marry the young girl. Sive loves a young man named Liam. Despite Sive's objections, she is being forced to marry the old man. Pats and Carthalawn are two neighbours who have been drinking with the Glavins. As this extract begins, it is discovered that Sive has gone missing.

Mena: *(Re-entering hysterically.)* She's gone! There's a bundle of clothes under the quilts where she should be lying. She's after stealing away on us!

Thomasheen: *(Seizes her by the arm roughly.)* What are you screeching about? Catch a hould of yourself.

Mena: She's gone, I tell you! The window of her room is open!

Thomasheen: Did she take baggage with her?

Mena: No! … No! … Nothing! Not even a shoe for her feet.

Thomasheen: Would she have stolen around to the old woman's room? *(Mena breaks from his grasp and hurries to Nanna's room to look in.)*

208

Thomasheen:	(loudly) Well? Is she there?
Mike:	(Stands up.) Where could she have gone at this hour of the night, without a shoe or a coat on her?
Pats:	There was something a while ago and we coming up from the cross.
Thomasheen:	Out with it! What?
Pats:	(frowningly) It may be that my eyes would be fooling me but I thought I saw the figure of a girl flashing across the bog near the end of the cutaway where the deep holes do be. I thought it might be a shadow.
Mena:	(Composed again.) And why didn't you say so when you came?
Pats:	How was I to know if the sight of my eyes was going or coming? It was only now that you talk about the girl that I think it might have been the girl, Sive.
Thomasheen:	You oul bacock! You oul' twisted bacock. Damn well you knew!
Pats:	I did not, and what is it to me if all the people of the parish ran over the bog in the middle of the night with bare feet.
Mena:	What if she fell into a hole … Oh, my God! (She shrieks at Mike.) Find her! Find her! … Hurry yourself!
Mike:	I'll get a lantern in the stable … (Mena rushes to the room by the fireplace and returns almost immediately with the rubber waders. Mike kicks off his shoes and pulls on the waders.)
Thomasheen:	I will go with you.
Seán Dotá:	I will go along with ye.
Mena:	Stay, Seán! I will not stay here alone by myself. Stay, somebody. Stay with me, I won't be alone.
Liam Scuab:	Show light! … Show light! … Leave open the door … I am coming over the bog.

(Thomasheen opens the door fully, Mena hurries with the oil lamp to the door, Mike hurries to the door. All exchange frightened glances.

They retreat from the door as Liam draws near. Their faces are horrified as they stand back.

Enter Liam. He is bareheaded and his clothes are wet. His face is ghastly pale. In his arms he carries Sive. Her hair is plastered to her head and her slight body hangs limp in Liam's arms. Liam advances without looking left or right. At the table he stops.

Pats comes forward and with his stick sweeps the table clean. The ware clatters on the ground breaking the silence. Reverently Liam lays the motionless body on the table.

The water drips on the floor from both Liam and Sive. Liam folds Sive's hand across her breast. Mena replaces the lamp)

Liam:	A cloth to dry her hair!

(Mena hands Liam a cloth. Thomasheen edges in to look at the body, then horrified, edges slyly away and exits, looking around him furtively. He is noticed only by Seán Dotá who follows him, backing, sneaking to the door. Seán exits.)

Liam:	(tearfully) I saw her running across the bog with only the little frock against the cold of the night. She ran like the wind and she letting cries out of her that would rend your heart. (Filled with sorrow.) I called after her but she would not stop. She took her own life. It was a while before I found her. The poor tormented child.
Mena:	Drowned, dead. (Liam turns suddenly on Mena, blazing with anger.)

Liam: *(cries in anguish)* You killed her! You … you … you … you killed her. That the hand of Jesus may strike you dead where you stand. You heartless wretch that haunted the poor little girl to the grave. *(Mena retreats, shocked, before him, her hand stupidly covering her mouth.)*

Liam: *(shrieks)* Go away! … Go away! You are polluting the pure spirit of the child with your nearness. Go away, witch! *(Liam raises the towel clenched in his fist to strike Mena. Mena hurries away back to her room, Liam begins to dry Sive's hair with the cloth, lovingly and with care.)*

Liam: The beautiful hair of her! *(He takes her hand.)* The lovely silky white of her!

Mike: *(stupidly, idiotically)* The priest … we must go for the priest … she must have the priest … Holy ground … she must be buried in holy ground … the priest … I must go for the priest. *(Liam gives Mike a scalding look.)*

Liam: Go for the priest then! … Go on! … Go! *(Mike siezes Liam by the two hands.)*

Mike: I can't go alone! … There's no luck in going for a priest alone. You know the old saying … *(Mike is foolish, babbling now. Liam shakes off Mike's hands violently. He seizes Mike by the hand and drags him to the door.)*

Liam: Come on! … I'll lead you past where she was drowned. You'll be on the tar road then. You'll find company. *(They both go out leaving Pats and Carthalawn alone with Sive. After a moment Carthalawn goes forward and touches Sive's face with his hand. His face is sad as he looks at her. After a few seconds Pats taps with his stick and Carthalawn draws away slowly. Both men stand to attention. Then, gently, the stick taps, the knuckles very gently tap the bodhrán to slow time. Slow of voice and tenderly Carthalawn sings. Pats looks at him tenderly.)*

Carthalawn: *(singing)*   Oh, come all good men and true,
A sad tale I'll tell to you
All of a maiden fair, who died this day;
Oh, they drowned lovely Sive,
She would not be a bride
And they laid her for to bury in the clay.

(They turn slowly and march slowly in step through the door, Carthalawn still singing gently.)

Carthalawn: *(singing)*   Oh, come all good men and true
A sad tale I'll tell to you
All of a maiden fair, who died this day;
Oh, they murdered lovely Sive,
She would not be a bride
And they laid her dead, to bury in the clay.

(The singing fades, slowly, slowly, as the light fades in the kitchen. Nanna, in the faint light, comes slowly from her room and goes to where Sive is lying. She bows her head over the dead body and weeps silently. The singing fades altogether.)

[Final Curtain]

1. How does Mena react when she realises Sive is missing?

2. How do you know that it is dangerous for Sive to be crossing the bog at night?

3. What is Liam's reaction to Sive's death? Who does he blame?

4. How do you know that Mike is religious?

5. Do you think that Pats and Carthalawn are saddened by Sive's death? Explain your answer fully.

6. If you were a detective investigating Sive's death, what questions would you ask?

7. How do you think Mena feels at the end of the play? **PQE**

8. How do you think this ending would affect an audience?

9. What kind of lighting and music would you use if you were directing this play? **PQE**

10. What did you notice about the way the characters spoke in this extract? **PQE**

Write a list of the sound effects you would have off-stage during this scene.

OR

Improvise a death scene. Imagine you have been murdered by poison, dagger or bullet, and that you only have time to say one sentence before you die. What would you say? Act out your death scene for the class.

OR

Imagine you are the murderer from the above improvisation. You are overwhelmed with guilt. Write a confession note for the police.

DON'T FORGET THAT:

The **opening** of a play, TV programme or film has to catch our attention. For example, in *A First Confession*, the way Nora and Jackie fight catches our attention. We also want to keep watching to see what will happen to Jackie.

When we watch a play we are introduced to various **characters.** We listen to what they say, watch what they do and hear what other people say about them. For example, in *Blood Brothers*, we see what kind of boys Mickey and Edward are from they way they talk and act, but we also hear about Sammy.

Most plays and films contain **conflict.** When we watch people fight, we don't know what will happen next and so we have to keep watching. This is called tension or suspense. For example, in *The Field*, we do not know what the Bull McCabe and his son are going to do to William.

People like films and plays which make them laugh. This is why **humour** is an important part of drama. For example, in *Skungpoomery*, we laugh at PC Wibble because we would all be embarrassed if our mothers behaved like his.

How a play is **staged** and where it is **set** help the writer to tell the story and the audience to believe what they see on stage. *The Silver Sword* is set during World War II, and the story would not make sense without the use of **props** like the sword, the kitten and the treasure box.

The **closing scene** is often the most exciting and dramatic moment. For example, in *Sive*, the main character's death ends the play in a tragic way.

5 Tell Me a Story

In this chapter you will learn:

- Why the opening of a story is important

- How to identify who is telling the story (the narrator)

- How to figure out the main message or theme behind a story

- Why suspense and tension help you to enjoy stories

- How to write good reviews of stories

I Am David

Anne Holm

This novel is about the journey of a boy called David. He escapes from a concentration camp. This story is probably set during the Cold War but we are never told this and it could easily take place anywhere in the world today.

The opening of a novel introduces us to the main character and immediately shows us the problems he or she faces. It also makes us ask questions so that we will read further to find out the answers.

David lay quite still in the darkness, listening to the men's low muttering. But this evening he was aware of their voices only as a vague meaningless noise in the distance, and he paid no attention to what they were saying.

'You must get away tonight,' the man had told him. 'Stay awake so that you're ready just before the guard's changed. When you see me strike a match, the current will be cut off and you can climb over – you'll have half a minute for it, no more.'

In his mind's eye David saw once again the grey bare room he knew so well. He saw the man and was conscious, somewhere in the pit of his stomach, of the hard knot of hate he felt whenever he saw him. The man's eyes were small, repulsive, light in colour, their expression never changing; his face was gross and fat. David had known him all his life, but he never spoke to him more than was barely necessary to answer his questions; and though he had known his name for as long as he could remember, he never said anything but 'the man' when he spoke about him or thought of him. Giving him a name would be like admitting that he knew him; it would place him on an equal footing with the others.

But that evening he had spoken to him. He had said, 'And if I don't escape?'

The man had shrugged his shoulders. 'That'll be none of my business. I have to leave here tomorrow, and whatever my successor may decide to do about you, I shan't be able to interfere. But you'll soon be a big lad, and there's need in a good many places for those strong enough to work.'

David knew only too well that those other places would not be any better than the camp where he now was. 'And if I get away without being caught, what then?' he had asked.

'Just by the big tree in the thicket that lies on the road out to the mines, you'll find a bottle of water and a compass. Follow the compass southwards till you get to Salonica, and then when no one's looking go on board a ship and hide. You'll have to stay hidden while the ship's at sea, and you'll need the water. Find a ship that's bound for Italy, and when you get there go north till you come to a country called Denmark – you'll be safe there.'

David had very nearly shown his astonishment, but he controlled himself, and hiding his feelings merely said, 'I don't know what a compass is.'

The man had shown him one, telling him that the four letters indicated north, south, east and west, and that the needle, which swung freely, always pointed in the same direction. Then he had added, 'The half minute the current's cut off is intended for you. If you try to take anyone with you, you can be sure that neither of you will get away. And now clear off before you're missed.'

David did not know what possessed him to say it – he had never asked the man for anything, partly because he knew it would be of no use, but chiefly because he would not – when you hated someone, you did not ask him for anything. But tonight he had done it: when he reached the door, he turned around, and looking straight into that coarse heavy face said, 'I'd like a piece of soap.'

For a moment there had been complete silence in that bare grey room. Then the man picked up a cake of soap that lay by the side of the wash-basin in the corner and threw it on the table. All he said was, 'Now go.'

So David had gone, as quickly as it was possible to go without appearing to be in a hurry.

The mens' muttering was fainter now – some of them must have fallen asleep. The camp's latest arrival was still talking. David recognised his voice because it was less flat and grating than the others. Whenever the newcomer dozed off to sleep, he was seized with a nightmare, and then they would all wake up again. The night before, this had happened just before the guard was changed, but if he took longer to fall asleep this evening, then it might be possible for David to slip out before the others were wakened again.

David was not yet sure whether he would make the attempt. He tried to work out why the man had told him to do it. It was certainly a trap: just as he was climbing over, the searchlight would suddenly swing round and catch him in its beam, and then they would shoot. Perhaps something pleasant was going to happen tomorrow and the man wanted him shot first. David had always known the man hated him, just as much as David hated *him* in return. On the other hand, nothing pleasant had ever yet happened in the camp that David could remember, and he was now twelve years old – it said so on his identity-card.

And then quite suddenly David decided he would do it. He had turned it over in his mind until his head was in a whirl and he still could not understand why the man had told him to escape. Suppose it was a trap and they shot him, it would all be over quickly anyway. If you were fired at while trying to escape, you would be dead within a minute. Yes, David decided to try.

There could not be many minutes left now. Over in the guard-room he could hear them moving about and getting dressed, and he could hear the guard yawning as his pace grew slower. Then came the sound of new steps and David pressed himself even more closely against the wall. It was the man; the faint sleepy yellow light from the guard-room shone for a moment on his face as he passed the window. He went up to the guard, and David suddenly felt quite empty inside and was sure that he would be unable to move when the time came. Then he saw before him the endless succession of days, months and years that would pass if he did not. The waiting would kill him in the end,

but it might take years. And it would grow worse and worse, all the time: David clenched his teeth so hard that he felt the muscles of his throat grow taut. Then the man struck a match.

Nineteen, twenty … the half minute would be up when he had counted slowly to thirty … David set his foot in a gap higher up the barbed wire … When would the searchlight come? They could not be certain of hitting him in the dark … and if they did not hurry he would be over.

A moment later he had touched the ground on the other side, and as he ran he said angrily to himself, 'What a fool you are! There's plenty of ground to cover yet – all this great flat stretch without so much as a stump of a tree for shelter. They'll wait till you've nearly reached the thicket … they'll think it more amusing if you believe you've almost got to safety.'

Why didn't they hurry up? The thought pounded through his head as every moment he expected to see the ground lit up in front of him. Then he stopped. He would run no more. When the beam of light caught him, they should see him walking away quite calmly. Then they would not enjoy it so much, they would feel cheated. The thought filled David with triumph.

When he was little, it had been his most burning desire to get the better of them, especially of the man. And now he would! They would be forced to shoot him as they watched him walking quietly away and taking no notice of them!

David was so taken up with his victory over them that he had gone a dozen yards past the spot where the thicket hid him from the camp before he realised that no one had fired. He stopped short. What could have happened? He turned, found a place where the thicket was thin enough to peer through and looked across at the low buildings outlined against the dark sky, like an even darker smudge of blackness. He could faintly hear the tread of the guard, but it came no nearer and sounded no different from usual, only farther off. Nothing at all appeared different.

David frowned in the darkness and stood for a moment undecided: it couldn't possibly…? He trotted on, following the edge of the thicket towards the big tree, running faster the nearer he got, and when he reached the tree he threw himself down on the ground, searching frantically with his hands round the trunk.

There was the bundle. David leaned up against the tree shivering with cold although it was not cold at all. The bundle was a piece of cloth wrapped round something and tied in a knot. He fumbled with the knot, but his fingers were clumsy and would not respond – and then he suddenly realised that he dared not undo it. There would be something dangerous inside the bundle … He tried to gather his thoughts together sufficiently to think what it might be, but his imagination did not get beyond a bomb.

It would make little difference, he though desperately – a bullet or a bomb: it would soon be over, either way. Frantically, his fingers awkward, he struggled with the knot.

But there was no bomb in the cloth. It was a square handkerchief tied cross-wise over a bottle of water and a compass, just as the man had said. He barely managed to turn aside before he was sick.

Afterwards he felt carefully all round the square-shaped bundle. A bottle, a compass – there was something else. David's eyes had grown accustomed to the darkness: in the bundle there were also a box of matches, a large loaf of bread and a pocket knife.

So the man had intended him to escape after all! A search-party would be sent out for him in the morning, but not before. The night was his, and it was up to him to make the most of it.

All this had taken only a few minutes, but to David it felt like hours. His hand closed tightly round the soap – he had not let go of it for a moment since he first got it. He recalled the hours he had spent that evening lying on his plank-bed listening to the muttered conversation of the men and thinking over what the man had said. He remembered, too, that it would be only a matter of time before he was caught again; but that, like everything else, no longer seemed important. All that mattered now was his bundle and the freedom of the night that lay ahead. Slowly he tucked the piece of soap into a corner of the handkerchief, laid the bottle, bread and knife on top, tied the ends together, took a firm grip on the knot and looked at the compass in his hand.

Then he ran.

1. How does David show that he hates the man?

2. What instructions does the man give to David?

3. What does the fact that David asks for soap suggest to you about his character?

4. Why does David decide that he should try to escape even though he believes that it is all a trap?

5. What age is David?

6. Why does David start walking when he is over the fence? What does this tell us about him?

7. Why do you think David gets sick?

8. What is in the bundle that David finds?

9. List the stages of David's escape.

10. Do you think David's escape will be a success?

Using the list you made when answering question 9, draw a graph charting David's feelings during the different stages of his escape.

determined

relieved

sad/worried

Stages of escape

OR

Imagine that you are the camp commandant. Write the letter that you would send to headquarters explaining David's escape.

OR

Find the opening to a good book or story that you have read before. Bring it into the class and explain why you think this opening is good.

11. Read the opening sentence again: 'David lay quite still in the darkness, listening to the men's low muttering.' What does this line tell us? What kind of **atmosphere** does it create?

12. Where does this story seem to be set? Why is this **setting** so important?

13. Has this extract made you ask yourself any questions? Write them down.

14. What do you think will happen next?

15. What is your first reaction to this book? Do you think it is a good opening to a novel?

Atmosphere is the feeling created by the description in a story.

The setting is the place and time where and when the story is occuring.

Safe

Kate Hanney

I'd only gone to school in the first place to get the 'Education Welfare Officer' off my back. He'd been round to the house again, acting all serious and talking about legal action. At first, I was going to ignore him like usual, but my mom got the face on, and I thought the best way to keep them both happy was to just turn up every now and again. So the next morning, I went.

It was all OK until French. I hated French – oh I know everybody does – but I really couldn't stand it. Our usual teacher wasn't too bad with me though. She, like most of the others, sort of knew I wasn't going to do much because I didn't see the point.

And I was never going to be a brain surgeon was I? And I really didn't see what difference a couple of GCSEs were going to make to my life. She understood this, and she pretty much left me alone. But that Friday we had a cover teacher. I knew him a bit, he'd been in some of our lessons before; but he didn't know me, not well enough to realise when to back off anyway.

It started from the minute I walked through the door. It was the second lesson of the day, and we didn't have a break between that and the first. So it was always a bit difficult: leaving lesson one, trying to get twos on a fag, and then not being late for the next lesson. Well I was a bit late that day, only a couple of minutes, but it was enough to wind him up.

'What's your name?' he snapped.

mardy –
awkward, bad-
tempered

I told him, and he made the 'Ah' sound. The 'Ah' meant he recognised my name; he knew now that I was one of those lads who hardly ever attended, and when I did, I always managed to get my name on the detention list. He shook his head and sighed; the look on his face was so dirty that he'd have needed bleach to get it off.

'Well, what do you think you're playing at, turning up at this time?'

He was being right mardy, and he didn't give me the chance to answer the first question before he went babbling on with the next.

'Who do you think you are, blah, blah, blah… disturbing the lesson, blah, blah… you'll make the time up at break, blah, blah, blah.'

OK, OK, I thought, staying calm. It's only a couple of minutes, I can put up with that.

I tried hard to ignore him and made my way to an empty chair at the back.

The next thing it was my jacket. We're not supposed to wear coats during the lessons, but it was freezing in that classroom and I only had a T-shirt on underneath. Sometimes I could get away with

The narrator is the person telling the story. In *Safe* there is a first-person narrator. A boy named Danny is telling the story from his point of view. He is also a character in the story.

leaving it on. But not that day; Mr Supply Teacher was going to follow the rules to the letter.

'Remove the coat as well,' he shouted, before I'd even sat down.

'OK, give me a chance,' I said.

'Don't speak to me like that,' he said. 'Just do it!'

I knew he was being all cocky and going over the top, but I decided to let him. I preferred to keep quiet if I could, so I sat down and took my jacket off. The cold made me shiver.

1. Why did Danny go back to school?

2. Why does he get into trouble?

3. What does the teacher give out to Danny about?

4. What do we learn about Danny's life outside school towards the end of the extract?

5. Why does Danny say he has no interest in school? **PQE**

6. How does Danny know the cover teacher recognises his name?

7. Do you think the teacher is fair to Danny? Why or why not? **PQE**

8. Would you like to read more of this book?

Write a letter to Danny giving your opinion about the situation and perhaps including some advice to help him deal with life in school.

OR

Write the report that the cover teacher will give to the Principal requesting Danny's detention. **R**

OR

Try to come up with the most outrageous excuse you can think of for being late or not having a pen. (Your teacher might be able to suggest some examples!)

There is a saying that *'Schooldays are the best days of your life'*. Get into groups and decide if you agree or disagree with this. Come up with reasons for your opinion and one member of the group will report back to the class.

Christopher

Eoin Colfer

The main message of a story is called its theme. Read the next story and think about what the writer is trying to say to us.

Marco dreamed of lying in fat green grass and gazing at blue sky. Sometimes the dream was so solid in his mind that he thought it must have actually happened. In another life maybe.

A thrown spool of thread knocked his forehead.

'You dreaming about grass again?'

Christopher. Of course. The Kenyan boy's smile was white in his dark face.

'Grass? Grass like fat worms?'

'Caterpillars, stupido,' corrected Marco.

Christopher frowned. 'Cat hair peelers? You are stupido, Marco baby.'

Marco chuckled twice. It took a lot to drag two chuckles out of a person in this place but Christopher could do it.

'You are the stupido, Christopher baby. And you stink like the backside of a sick dog.'

Now Christopher chuckled. 'Backside of a sick dog. This is a prince among insults.'

Heavy footsteps creaked on the floorboards and the boys stopped their joking. Bluto was on the workfloor. The factory foreman honked into the phone for a minute then hung up, muttering about whatever new problem the phone call had brought him. This was dangerous time. Bluto fined people when he was upset.

Marco hunched low into his work, shutting out the universe. This was what Bluto wanted to see in his employees: a good work ethic. On this Sunday Marco was stitching gold wings on the pockets of fake Nike shorts. The wing was the adopted symbol of the AC Milan striker, Costas Andioni.

sweatshop – unhealthy working environment, usually a factory

'Andioni breaks his leg and we're gonna be picking these wings out with our teeth,' Christopher had whispered just loudly enough for everyone to hear, earning himself a clout on the ear and another visit to the office.

Mrs M had left the door open so the workers could hear what happened to smartmouths.

'This ain't no sweatshop, Kenya,' she had shouted, her shrill voice rising to the concrete ceiling. 'You're free to go anytime you want. You want to go, please go. You going, Kenya?'

Christopher shook his head, chin so low it touched his chest.

They have broken him, thought Marco. Even brave, shining Christopher.

221

But when Christopher returned to his bench the first thing he did was to ask whether Marco had farted.

Not broken. Still Christopher.

Marco never offered backchat as he could not afford to be docked an hour's pay. Bluto loved to dock wages. Christopher said that whatever Bluto took from you, he kept for himself to buy rare Pokemon cards for his collection. Everyone pulled their weight at Marco's home, even the twins helped to make the foil roses that Mother sold at the city's traffic lights.

'Speedy, Mr Bluto,' Marco would say, hating the man even as he smiled. 'Just the way you like it.'

And so he worked that day. Wing after wing. Gold thread on the inside, red flames feathered around the border. Marco worked without a break until dusk, until his backbone was a glowing rod and his fingers were claws.

Eventually, he leaned back and sighed, his breath pluming like chimney smoke. Mrs M always turned off the heat around midday, claiming that the workers' own industry should keep them warm.

Marco pushed back his chair, tugged at his cushion to make sure it was tied down securely, and walked stiffly towards the bathroom past the 30 or so workers.

In spite of the factory's chill, a dense smell clogged the building. There was bleach in the mix, and sweat, rubber and oil. Though he knew it was merely a mix of chemicals, Marco imagined the smell was alive. He could use this in one of his stories.

Marco often wrote stories, most featuring Quantum Boy (Marco himself) and his sidekick, Dreadlock (Christopher of course). Quantum Boy zipped through time getting himself entangled in famous historical adventures and Dreadlock was always on hand with a witty comment at the right time. For example: This time you have come up short, Napoleon.

Marco ducked quickly inside the cramped bathroom. He did not pull the bulb cord, because then Mr Bluto would see the light leaking out under the door and come to hurry him along.

The bathroom was colder than the rest of the building because it wasn't really part of the building. There was a a gap one block wide all the way around where the breeze blocks had subsided from the factory proper. The wind whistled through and froze the toilet seat.

And while Marco warmed the seat with his palm, he did not notice the click-clack of Bluto's approaching footsteps. And because there was no light on the floor, Bluto presumed the bathroom was empty.

He barrelled into the cramped space backwards, shouting into his phone. 'I said Tropical Mega Battle, gold edition, you idiot. Not bronze. I won't pay a penny for bronze.'

Bluto did not realise Marco was there until he sat on him. Even then he did not know that it was Marco, because if he had he surely would not have run onto the work floor with his trousers in his hand screaming: 'Toilet monster! It bit me. They are real. I knew it. I knew it.'

The experience was not pleasant for Marco either. One second his life did not seem to be in any immediate danger, and the next there was a sudden overpowering smell of sweat and cheese and his face was mashed by back fat.

Marco stumbled into the factory, squinting and gasping like a prisoner released from his dungeon. 'Sorry,' he coughed, knowing that whatever had happened would be his fault. 'I'm sorry, sir. I must hurry back to work.'

Bluto lurched forward, grabbing Marco's shoulder.

'Tell them, boy. You must have felt it.' Then Bluto stuttered to a halt as the truth became clear. It had been Marco in the bathroom with the lights off. Only Marco.

'No toilet monster,' he breathed, calming himself with gulps of air. 'Just a boy.'

And for a moment he was happy, then the red tinge of embarrassment coloured his cheeks. By now every worker in the factory had gathered around – even Mrs M had come from her office to check on the disturbance. She stood, wrapped in her knee-length puffa jacket, glaring at the foreman.

'When I was a child,' explained Bluto. 'My brother told me stories of a monster who lived in the toilet bowl.' It was ridiculous, even to his own ears.

'This boy!' he shouted, hoisting his trousers with one hand. 'Skulking in the bathroom with the light off. He must be docked! Fired!'

Christopher piped up from the throng of workers. 'The toilet monster. He is the one who must be fired.' A few workers tittered but not Bluto. 'Shut your mouth, Kenya. This boy must go.'

'But if Marco goes, who will stitch Andioni's wings?' asked Christopher. 'The toilet monster. His fingers are clumsy and he will drip on the material.'

More laughter now, even Mrs M's mouth was twitching at one corner.

'Please, Mrs M,' pleaded Bluto. 'Fire him now.'

Christopher contorted his face and limbs in a hilarious impression of a dull monster trying to sew.

'Arrrrrgh. Di work berry difficult for poor toilet monster.'

Bluto dropped Marco and charged at Christopher. The other workers clapped and whooped as Christopher easily dodged the foreman, weaving between the machines. The fun might have lasted for longer, had not Mrs M anticipated Christopher's route and snagged him by the ear as he shot around a corner.

'That's the end of your little game, Kenya,' she snapped. 'Into the office with you.'

223

Bluto was still in attack mode, but Mrs M froze him with a single pointed finger. 'And you! Prepare my peppermint tea. And in future, whistle before entering the bathroom. Everyone knows that the toilet monster cannot bear whistling.'

'A good joke, Mrs M,' said Christopher, still smiling.

Mrs M shrank his smile with another tug on the ear, dragging the skinny boy towards her office, where he would surely be fired.

Marco did not know what to do. Quantum Boy would blast Mrs M into the dinosaur age, but Marco had no special powers. He was a scared boy who still hadn't used the bathroom. Though he felt a little guilty, Marco backed into the bathroom, remembering to switch on the light. In the corner of his eye something moved. It was Mrs M. Her office window could be clearly seen through the gap between bathroom and factory floor.

Before Marco realised what he was doing, his arm was through the gap, seeming to pull the rest of him after it.

It was a tight squeeze, but Marco sucked in his ribcage, flattened his nose and managed to inch through the gap until he emerged into the factory yard. The sky was wrong. Were there should be the dark blue of night, there were orange bellied clouds, reflecting the city's street lights.

Go back, whispered Marco's good sense. Go back.

But he did not.

The window blinds were old and missing several slats so Marco's view was barely obstructed. He made a funnel with his hands and looked through it to the room inside.

Mrs M was behind her desk shouting at Christopher, who sat in a wooden chair facing her. She shouted and pounded the desk, making the pens jump.

I must call out to him, thought Marco. Share the blame. Perhaps Mrs M would fine us both and fire neither.

But then Marco noticed that something was not right. Mrs M smiled and even winked at Christopher who did not seem in the least afraid. As a matter of fact he seemed comfortable and relaxed, propping his knees on the desk and helping himself to some peanuts from a bowl.

Marco moved further along to a spot where the pane was cracked and a dagger shaped sliver of glass had fallen out.

'Another incident like this and you will be let go, Kenya!' he heard Mrs M say.

'Thank you, Madam,' Christopher said, his white teeth like rows of chewing gum. 'I will be a good worker.'

It was all fake, Marco realised. For the benefit of those listening on the factory floor.

Mrs M spoke again, this time in quiet tones. 'You go too far with Bluto,' she said. 'Your job is to keep the workers happy. Happy workers are hard workers.'

'Bluto was scaring Marco,' said Christopher. 'He is the best one we have.'

Mrs M was impressed by such wisdom. 'You are right, dear Christopher. If Marco had gone, 10 more would follow him and the Andioni order would never be finished on time.' She opened her desk drawer and took out a few notes. 'A small bonus for my Trojan horse.'

Christopher took the money and tucked it into his sock. 'You should tell Bluto to leave Marco alone. He is soft but I like him.'

'I will tell him. Now, you go back to work.'

'Five more minutes – a can of Pepsi?'

Mrs M smiled almost tenderly. 'One can. Five minutes, then you go out of here crying like a baby.'

Christopher pushed out his bottom lip.

'No one cries like Christopher,' he said. Then in a typical Christopher motion he popped out of the chair like a circus acrobat and trotted across to a small fridge on the floor. He selected a cola and stretched on the ground to drink it.

'Drink slowly,' Mrs M chided. 'Or you will give yourself tummy ache.' Christopher's reply was a gentle burp.

Marco turned away from the window. His friend's job was safe, that much was clear. But was his friend his friend?

Dreadlock is gone, he realised. There is only Quantum Boy now.

Marco felt cold and betrayed. Christopher had been masquerading as their comedian, when all the time he was under Mrs M's wing. Even so, I still laughed. Does it matter why he jokes?

It did matter, Marco decided. Christopher's jokes were like glossy red apples with black sludge at their core. He would not laugh again.

Marco felt sick to his stomach and wished that he could just go home. But he knew he must return to the factory. But before he went back inside, Marco allowed himself one last longing look at the lights and life of the city beyond. His mother was out there somewhere, selling foil roses at the traffic lights of east London.

1. What is Marco dreaming of?

2. What is the factory foreman's name?

3. What work are Marco and Christopher doing?

4. Why is Christopher called into the office and who gives out to him?

5. What superhero names does Marco give himself and Christopher?

6. What happens when Marco goes to the toilet?

7. How does Christopher get into trouble for a second time?

8. Why is Marco shocked when he looks through the window of the office?

9. How does Marco feel about Christopher's actions?

10. Did you expect this story to be set in London? Why or why not?

14. How did this story make you feel?

15. What do you think is the main message in this story? Choose the word below that you think best sums up the theme. Explain your choice.

Friendship   Exploitation   Deception

Christopher lets Marco down in this story. Write about a time that you felt let down.

OR

Draw a picture of what you think Quantum Boy and his sidekick Dreadlock should look like.

OR

Do some research with your class on the problem of sweatshops and slave labour. Write a letter or send an email to the Minister for Foreign Affairs outlining your views on this issue.

11. What evidence is there in the story to tell us that Marco and Christopher are working in a sweatshop? **P Q E**

12. Write down three words that you would use to describe Marco. Find examples from the story to explain why you would pick these words.

13. Even though this is a sad story there are moments of humour in it. Pick out a moment in the story that you thought was funny.

Eoin Colfer wrote this story as part of a collection inspired by the Universal Declaration of Human Rights. The Human Right he chose was:

Everyone has the right to rest and leisure, including reasonable limitation of working hours and periodic holidays with pay.

Using your CSPE book, or the internet, research some of the other Human Rights in this Declaration. Have a class discussion about which ones you think are most important.

Scorpia

Anthony Horowitz

The siren was warning that there was going to be a flood. Venice has an alarm system in place all year round. The city stands at sea level and because of the wind and the atmospheric pressure, there are frequent storm surges. These cause water from the Adriatic to pour into the Venice lagoon, with the result that the canals break their banks and whole streets and squares simply disappear for several hours. Cold black water was bubbling up into the room even now. How high would it go? Alex didn't need to ask. The stains on the walls went all the way up to the ceiling. The water would rise over him and he would struggle helplessly, unable to save himself, until he drowned. Eventually the level would fall again and they would clear out his body, perhaps dumping it in the lagoon.

He leapt to his feet and ran to the door, slamming his hands against it. He was shouting too, although he knew it was hopeless. Nobody came. Nobody cared. He surely wasn't the first to end up locked in here. Ask too many questions, go into rooms where you had no right to be, and this was the result.

The water was rising steadily. It must have been five centimetres deep already. The floor had disappeared. There were no windows, and the door was rock solid. There was only one possible way out of here and Alex was almost too afraid to try it. But one of the planks was loose. Maybe there was some sort of well or large pipe underneath. After all, he reasoned, there had to be some way for the water to come in.

And it was gushing in now, more quickly than ever. Alex hurried back down the stairs. The water level was well over his ankles, almost reaching his knees. He made a quick calculation. At this rate the room would be completely submerged in about three minutes. He ripped off the waistcoat and threw it aside. He wouldn't need that now. He waded forward, searching with his feet for the loose plank. He remembered that it was somewhere in the middle and soon found it, stubbing his toe against one side of the opening. He knelt down, the water now circling his waist. He wasn't even sure he could squeeze through. And if he did, what would he find on the other side?

He tried to feel with his hands. There was an upsurge of water right beneath him. This was the source of the inflow. The water was coming up directly from some sort of opening. So this had to be the way out. The only question was – could he do it? He would have to force himself, head first, through the tiny gap, find the opening and swim into it. If he got stuck he would drown upside down. If the passage was blocked he would never make it back again. He was kneeling in front of the worst of deaths imaginable. And the water was creeping up his spine, pitiless and cold.

Bitter anger shivered through him. Was this the destiny that Yassen Gregorovich had promised him? Had he come to Venice simply for this? The sirens were still howling.

The water had covered the first two steps and were already lapping at the third. Alex cursed, then took several deep breaths, hyperventilating. When he had forced as much air into his lungs as he thought they could take, he toppled over and plunged head first through the hole.

The gap was barely big enough. He felt the edge of the wooden floorboards bite into his shoulders, but then he was able to use his hands to propel himself onward. He was utterly blind. Even if he had opened his eyes, the water would have been black. He could feel it pressing against his nostrils and lips. It was ice-cold and stinking. God! What a way to die. His stomach had passed through the opening but his hips were stuck. Alex twisted like a snake and the lower part of his body came free.

He was already running out of air. He wanted to turn and go back, but now fresh panic gripped him as he realised he was trapped inside some sort of tube with no room to go any way except down. His shoulders banged against solid brick. He kicked out with one leg and was rewarded with a stab of pain as his foot hit the wall that enclosed him. He felt the current swirling round his face and neck – ropes of water that wanted to bind him for ever in this black death. He became aware of the full horror of his situation now that there was no escape from it. No adult would have been able to get this far. It was only because he was smaller that he had been able to make his way into this well shaft or whatever it was. But there was no room for manoeuvre. The walls were already touching him on every side. If the tube became any narrower, he would be stuck fast.

He forced himself on. Forward and down, his hands groping ahead of him, dreading the metal bars that would tell him that Nile had been laughing at him from the start. His lungs were straining; the pressure was hammering at his chest. He tried not to panic, knowing it would only use up his air more quickly, but already his brain was screaming at him to stop, to breathe in, to give up and accept his fate. Forward and down. He could hold his breath for two minutes. And it couldn't have been more than a minute since he had taken the plunge. Don't give in! Just keep moving …

By now he must be ten or fifteen metres under the cellar floor. He reached out and whimpered as his knuckles struck brick. A few precious bubbles of air escaped between his lips and chased up his body, past his flailing legs. At first he thought he had come to a dead end. He opened his eyes for a split second. It made no difference at all. Open or closed, there was nothing to see: he was in pitch darkness. His heart seemed to stop beating. In that moment Alex experienced what it would be like to die.

But then his other hand felt the curve of the wall and he realised that at last the well shaft was bending. He had reached the bottom of an elongated J and somehow he had to get round the turn. Perhaps this was where it finally joined the canal. As it twisted, it tightened. As if the swirling water wasn't enough, Alex felt the brickwork close in on him, scratching his legs and chest. He knew he had very little air left. His lungs were straining and there was a giddy emptiness in his head. He was about to slide into unconsciousness. Well, that would come as a blessing. Maybe he would never feel the water rushing into his mouth and down his throat. Maybe he would be asleep before the end.

He turned the corner. His hands hit something – bars of some sort – and he was able to pull his legs round. Only then did he discover that his worst fears had been realised. He had come to the end of the well shaft but there was a metal barrier, a circular gate. He was holding it. There was no way out.

Tension occurs when the excitement in a story builds up and we know that something is going to happen …

DIVE IN!

1. What danger is Alex in during the first paragraph?

2. How long will it take for the room to become completely submerged?

3. What method of escape does Alex decide on?

4. How long can Alex hold his breath for?

5. Do you think he will succeed in escaping?

TAKE THE PLUNGE!

6. Reread the first paragraph in this extract. What details create **tension**? **P Q E**

7. Based on this extract what sort of a person do you think Alex is? **P Q E**

8. Did you think this extract was exciting? Why or why not?

WHY DON'T YOU…

If this extract was a scene in a film what sound effects or music tracks would you choose to accompany it? List the sound effects stating where and when you would use them. Name the song or piece of music that you would play in the background.

OR

Your town is about to flood. Write the instructions you would read over a loudspeaker system informing people of the danger, and telling them what to do.

OR

Alex faces the fear of drowning and of enclosed tunnels in this extract. What are your worst fears? Describe in detail the situation that you might have a phobia about.

THRASH IT OUT!

Make a list of your favourite tense moments from TV programmes, films or books. Compile a class top ten. Discuss what makes these moments stand out.

Private Peaceful

Michael Morpurgo

*Charlie and Tommo are two brothers. They are searching for their brother Big Joe.
Big Joe has special needs and he has been missing all night. Tommo is telling the story.*

I opened the church door and walked into the silent dark of the church. I brushed past the bell ropes, and eased open the little belfry door. I could hear Charlie shouting, 'Is he up there? Is he there?' I didn't answer. I began to climb the winding stairs. I'd been up into the belfry before, a while ago, when I was in Sunday school. I'd even sung up there in the choir one Ascension Day dawn, when I was little.

I dreaded those steps then and I hated them again now. The slit windows let in only occasional light. The walls were slimy about me, and the stairs uneven and slippery. The cold and the damp and the dark closed in on me and chilled me as I felt my way onwards and upwards. As I passed the silent hanging bells I hoped with all my heart that one of them would be ringing soon. Ninety-five steps I knew there were. With every step I was longing to reach the top, to breathe the bright air again, longing to find Big Joe.

The door to the tower was stiff and would not open. I pushed it hard, too hard, and it flew open, the wind catching it suddenly. I stepped out into the welcome warmth of day, dazzled by the light. At first glance I could see nothing. But then there he was. Big Joe was lying curled up under the shade of the parapet. He seemed fast asleep, his thumb in his mouth as usual. I didn't want to wake him too suddenly. When I touched his hand he did not wake. When I shook him gently by the shoulder he did not move. He was cold to my touch, and pale, deathly pale. I couldn't tell if he was breathing or not, and Charlie was calling up at me from below.

*parapet –
wall-like barrier*

I shook him again, hard this time, and screamed at him in my fear and panic. 'Wake up, Joe. For God's sake, wake up!' I knew then that he wouldn't, that he'd come up here to die. He knew you had to die to get to Heaven, and Heaven was where he wanted to be, to be with Bertha again, and Father too.

When he stirred a moment later, I could hardly believe it. He opened his eyes. He smiled. 'Ha, Tommo,' he said. 'Ungwee. Ungwee.' They were the most beautiful words I'd ever heard. I sprang to my feet and leaned out over the parapet. Charlie was down there on the church path looking up at me.

'We've found him, Charlie,' I called down. 'We've got him. He's up here. He's all right.'

Charlie punched the air and yahooed again and again. He yahooed even louder when he saw Big Joe standing beside me and waving. 'Charie!' he cried. 'Charie!'

Charlie hopped and limped into the church, and only moments later the great tenor bell rang out over the village, scattering the roosting pigeons from the tower, and sending them wheeling out over the houses, over the fields. Like the pigeons, Big Joe and I were shocked at the violence of the sound. It blasted our ears, sent a tremor through the tower that we felt through the soles of our feet. Alarmed at all this thunderous clanging, Big Joe looked suddenly anxious, his hands clapped over his ears. But when he saw me laughing he did the same. Then he hugged me, hugged me so tight I thought he was squeezing me half to death. And when he began singing *Oranges and Lemons,* I joined in, crying and singing at the same time.

> A climax is the moment that all the tension has been building up to. It is the most important, vital moment in a piece of writing.

1. How does Tommo feel about the staircase?

2. When he finds Big Joe, what does he think?

3. How does Charlie react when he hears that Big Joe has been found?

4. What does Charlie do to tell all the other searchers that Big Joe has been found?

5. How do we know Big Joe is happy to be found?

6. Pick out three details that help create a tense atmosphere in the first two paragraphs. **P Q E**

7. How does the writer keep the reader worried even after Joe has been found? **P Q E**

8. Re-read the definition of a **climax** at the beginning of this extract. Do you think this piece of writing is a good example? Why or why not? **P Q E**

Write a story with lots of tension, suspense and an exciting climax, *ending* with the words:

I stepped out into the welcome warmth of day, dazzled by the light.

Remember to:

- Decide on your setting – where and when your story will take place

- Create an atmosphere using good descriptive writing

- Plan in advance the beginning, middle and end of your story

- Include dialogue if necessary

OR

Charlie hated climbing the stairs of the bell-tower. Write a description, real or imagined, of a journey you really didn't want to make.

OR

Draw the storyboard you would prepare if you were going to film this extract. Include six pictures of the moments you think are most important. **R**

His First Flight

Liam O'Flaherty

The young seagull was alone on his ledge. His two brothers and his sister had already flown away the day before. He had been afraid to fly with them. Somehow when he had taken a little run forward to the brink of the ledge and attempted to flap his wings he became afraid. The great expanse of sea stretched down beneath, and it was such a long way down – miles down. He felt certain that his wings would never support him, so he bent his head and ran away back to the little hole under the ledge where he slept at night. Even when each of his brothers and his little sister, whose wings were far shorter than his own, ran to the brink, flapped their wings, and flew away, he failed to muster up courage to take that plunge which appeared to him so desperate. His father and mother had come around calling to him shrilly, upbraiding him, threatening to let him starve on his ledge unless he flew away. But for the life of him he could not move.

That was twenty-four hours ago. Since then nobody had come near him. The day before, all day long, he had watched his parents flying about with his brothers and sister, perfecting them in the art of flight, teaching them how to skim the waves and how to dive for fish. He had, in fact, seen his older brother catch his first herring and devour it, standing on a rock, while his parents circled around raising a proud cackle. And all the morning the whole family had walked about on the big plateau midway down the opposite cliff, taunting him with his cowardice.

A resolution is the way in which a story is wrapped up.

The sun was now ascending the sky, blazing warmly on his ledge that faced the south. He felt the heat because he had not eaten since the previous nightfall. Then he had found a dried piece of mackerel's tail at the far end of his ledge. Now there was not a single scrap of food left. He had searched every inch, rooting among the rough, dirt-caked straw nest where he and his brothers and sister had been hatched. He even gnawed at the dried pieces of spotted eggshell. It was like eating a part of himself.

upbraiding – giving out to

precipice – steep cliff

He had then trotted back and forth from one end of the ledge to the other, his grey body the colour of the cliff, his long grey legs stepping daintily, trying to find some means of reaching his parents without having to fly. But on each side of him the ledge ended in a sheer fall of precipice, with the sea beneath. And between him and his parents there was a deep, wide chasm. Surely he could reach them without flying if he could only move northwards along the cliff face? But then on what would he walk? There was no ledge, and he was not a fly. And above him he could see nothing. The precipice was sheer, and the top of it was perhaps farther away than the sea beneath him.

He stepped slowly out to the brink of the ledge, and, standing on one leg with the other hidden under his wing, he closed one eye, then the other, and pretended to be falling asleep. Still they took no notice of him. He saw his two brothers and his sister lying on the plateau dozing, with their heads sunk into their necks. His father was preening his feathers

on his white back. Only his mother was looking at him. She was standing on a little high hump on the plateau, her white breast thrust forward. Now and again she tore at a piece of fish that lay at her feet, and then scraped each side of her beak on the rock. The sight of the food maddened him. How he loved to tear food that way, scraping his beak now and again to whet it! He uttered a low cackle. His mother cackled too, and looked over at him.

'Ga, ga, ga,' he cried, begging her to bring him over some food. 'Gaw-ool-al,' she screamed back derisively. But he kept calling plaintively, and after a minute or so he uttered a joyful scream. His mother had picked up a piece of fish and was flying across to him with it. He leaned out eagerly, tapping the rock with his feet, trying to get nearer to her as she flew across. But when she was just opposite to him, abreast of the ledge, she halted, her legs hanging limp, he wings motionless, the piece of fish in her beak almost within reach of his beak. He waited a moment in surprise, wondering why she did not come nearer, and then, maddened by hunger, he dived at the fish. With a loud scream he fell outwards and downwards into space. His mother had swooped upwards. As he passed beneath her he heard the swish of her wings. Then a monstrous terror seized him and his heart stood still. He could hear nothing. But it only lasted a moment. The next moment he felt his wings spread outwards. The wind rushed against his breast feathers, then under his stomach and against his wings. He could feel the tips of his wings cutting through the air. He was not falling headlong now. He was soaring gradually downwards and outwards. He was no longer afraid. He just felt a bit dizzy. Then he flapped his wings once and he soared upwards. He uttered a joyous scream and flapped them again. He soared higher. He raised his breast and banked against the wind. 'Ga, ga, ga. Ga, ga, ga. Gaw-ool-ah.' His mother swooped past him, her wings making a loud noise. He answered her with another scream. Then his father flew over to him screaming. Then he saw his two brothers and sister flying around him curvetting and banking and soaring and diving.

Then he completely forgot that he had not always been able to fly, and commenced himself to dive and soar and curvet, shrieking shrilly.

derisively – mockingly

plaintively – sadly

curvet – frisk about

He was near the sea now, flying straight over it, facing straight out over the ocean. He saw a vast green sea beneath him, with little ridges moving over it, and he turned his beak sideways and crowed amusedly. His parents and his brothers and sister had landed on this green floor in front of him. They were beckoning to him, calling shrilly. He dropped his legs to stand on the green sea. His legs sank into it. He screamed with fright and attempted to rise again, flapping his wings. But he was tired and weak with hunger and he could not rise, exhausted by the strange exercise. His feet sank into the green sea, and then his belly touched it and he sank no farther. He was floating on it. And around him his family was screaming, praising him, and their beaks were offering him scraps of dog-fish.

He had made his first flight.

233

Dive In!

DIVE IN!

1. Why is the young seagull alone on the ledge?

2. What has his family been doing?

3. How does his mother trick him?

4. Does he enjoy flying when it happens?

5. Did you like the final line of the story?

TAKE THE PLUNGE!

6. In this story the seagull is described almost as if he were human. Can you find some examples of this?

7. How did you feel towards the seagull during this story? Choose one or more of the following words and explain why you felt that way:

   nervous, pity, annoyance, excitement, fear, pride, jealousy, happiness, impatient

   Complete your sentence like this:

   I felt nervous for the seagull because he didn't know if he would be able to fly, and yet if he didn't he would have starved.

8. Look back at the description of the seagull trying to find food on his ledge. What details caught your attention and why? **P Q E**

9. In your opinion, at what point does the climax of this story occur? **P Q E**

10. Did you enjoy this story? Why or why not?

WHY DON'T YOU...

Rewrite this story from the mother's point of view.

OR

Write a story based on one of the situations in these photos. Try to describe this moment as dramatically as possible.

DON'T FORGET THAT:

The **opening** of a novel introduces us to the main character and immediately shows us the problems he or she faces. It also makes us ask questions so that we will read further to find out the answers, for example, the beginning of *I Am David*.

The **narrator** is the person telling the story. In *Safe* there is a **first-person narrator**. A boy named Danny is telling the story from his **point of view** and he is also a character in the story.

The main message of a story is called its **theme**. For example, the theme of *Christopher* is that exploitation is wrong.

Tension occurs when the excitement in a story builds up and we know that something is going to happen. For example, we felt tension in *Scorpia* because we didn't know if Alex would survive.

A **climax** is the moment that all the tension has been building up to. It is the most important, vital moment in the story. For example, in *Private Peaceful*, it was the moment that Tommo realised his brother Big Joe was still alive.

The **resolution** is the way in which the story is wrapped up. For example, in *His First Flight*, the story ends with the seagull's triumphant first flight.

What Do You Think?

Writing a Book Review

1 INTRODUCE ...
- What you are going to write about.
- The **title** of the book.
- The **type** of book it is, e.g. horror, romance, drama, comedy, etc.

2 DESCRIBE ...
- **Where** and **when** the story takes place.
- Who the main **character** or characters are.
- The general outline of the **plot** *without spoiling the ending!*
- The main point or **message** of the book in one sentence, if possible.

3 JUDGE ...
- The main **strengths** and **weaknesses,** in your opinion.
- How much you liked or disliked the characters.
- How realistic the **dialogue** was.
- Whether the descriptions of the **relationships** were believable.
- Whether the book kept your interest or not. Were there elements of **suspense?**
- Whether the **ending** was satisfactory or not – *without giving it away!*
- The **language** to see if it was reader friendly or not and whether the **descriptions** were effective.

4 DECIDE ...
- Who you would give the book to and why.
- Whether the book is **suitable** for teenagers or younger children?
- What **type of reader** would enjoy this particular book?
- Who would not enjoy this book?

The facing page shows an example of a book review. ℝ

1 Loser by Jerry Spinelli is the story of Donald Zinkoff's journey through primary school. This sounds really boring but, in fact, it is an often hilarious, sometimes sad, description of childhood.

2 The story takes place in America in the present day. The main character, Donald Zinkoff, is an unusual little boy. He loves school! He gets excited when he learns to spell 'tintinnabulation', and he feels sad when he has to stay at home for three weeks. The other children think he is a 'loser' but by the end of the book something changes. This book gives us the message that it's alright to be different.

3 My favourite part of this book was the character of Zinkoff. At first I wasn't sure what to make of him but he gradually grew on me. Nothing tickles Zinkoff 'more than the sound of a funny word'. When he hears the invented word 'Jabip' he laughs for five minutes on the classroom floor, much to the bewilderment of his class and teacher. There are also other entertaining characters like Hector Binn, who is saving his ear wax to make a candle! The dialogue is very effective, using real children's language. For example, Zinkoff has to ask his teacher what 'represents' means. The relationship between Zinkoff and his parents is touching. They never judge him and don't care even when he does really badly in the sports day. Spinelli keeps the reader's interest right to the end of the book. We care about Zinkoff and want to know what will happen to him. The language in this book was very easy to read but it wasn't childish. My favourite description was of the giant Snickerdoodle cookie that Zinkoff baked, which was 'warm, soft and heavenly smelling'.

4 I would highly recommend this book to all readers but especially to people who have just finished primary school. This is because it will make you remember and laugh at some of the things you thought and did when you were little. The ending comes a bit suddenly and you would like to know more about Zinkoff's future.

Recommended Novels

Northern Lights
Philip Pullman

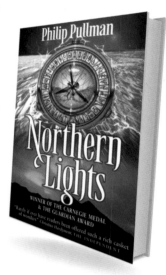

When Lyra's friend Roger disappears, she and her daemon Pantalaimon determine to find him. The quest that follows is full of strange terrors and high adventure. The first book in the highly successful trilogy.

Big Mouth and Ugly Girl
Joyce Carol Oates

Matt has a big mouth and Ursula is the 'ugly girl' in school, but when Matt is arrested on suspicion of having plans to blow up their High School it is Ursula who unexpectedly springs to his defence.

Inkheart
Cornelia Funke

A father reads books out loud to his daughter, and as he does so the characters come to life. This is a page-turning fantasy adventure, where good characters must battle against evil.

Across the Nightingale Floor
Lian Hearn

An epic story set in feudal Japan. Takeo is adopted by a Samurai warrior. Trained in the ways of the Samurai himself he has the opportunity to take revenge on the clan who killed his family. A novel full of exciting adventure and romance.

The Cinnamon Tree
Aubrey Flegg

Yola's life is changed completely when she steps on a landmine and loses her leg below the knee. She is now unmarriageable. She is sent to Ireland for treatment where she meets Fintan and she begins to realise the depth and strength of the international arms trade which is controlled by ruthless, powerful people who operate thousands of miles away from the conflicts. A novel that leaves you thinking.

The Alchemyst
Michael Scott

Nicholas Flamel is an alchemist who has discovered the secret to eternal life. The evil Dr John Dee plans to use this knowledge to destroy the world. Only Sophie and Josh Newman, two teenagers, can stop him. A brilliant fantasy adventure.

A Gathering Light
Jennifer Donnelly

A novel set in America at the turn of the century. The central character longs to escape from the farm where she lives, and the man that she is supposed to marry. A murder occurs which complicates her plans for escape.

Playing Against the Odds
Bernard Ashley

Chris has a crush on the new girl Fiona, but his classmates think she's a thief. Can he prove her innocence so he can go out with her?

The Amulet of Samarkand
Jonathan Stroud

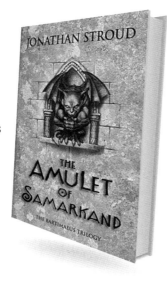

A twelve-year-old apprentice magician has some problems with a troublesome genie. A witty and modern take on fantasy fiction.

Wendy
Karen Wallace

This is the story of Peter Pan, told from Wendy's point of view. This book gives a new perspective to a well-known tale.

The Goose Girl
Shannon Hale

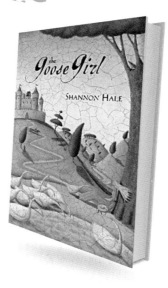

A fairy tale for all ages. Princess Ani is sent on a journey to her future husband. She escapes, disguised as a goose girl, and lives in the forest under her assumed identity. Adventures and danger follow.

The Looking Glass Wars
Frank Beddor

A dazzling new interpretation of Alice's Adventures in Wonderland. Alice has been hiding out in our world because of the danger of assassination, now it's time for her to go back to Wonderland!

The Boy in the Striped Pyjamas
John Boyne

A moving and poignant novel about an unlikely friendship during World War II, which takes the reader on a very unexpected journey.

Girls in Love
Jacqueline Wilson

Ellie, Magda and Nadine are the girls who are in love. Ellie's mother died when she was young and she lives with her dad, step-mum Anna and half-brother Eggs. She really misses her mother's advice when it comes to boys.

When her best friend Nadine gets a boyfriend Ellie feels under even more pressure. This is the first book in a series of three and in a humorous way looks at how tricky the love life of a teenager can be!

The Knife of Never Letting Go
Patrick Ness

This is a breathtakingly exciting novel about the dangerous choices of growing up. Todd Hewitt has grown up in a town filled with never-ending Noise where everyone can hear each other's thoughts. And then, just one month from his birthday, he discovers a spot of silence. Because of this discovery he becomes a boy on the run.

Bridge to Terabithia
Katherine Paterson

Jess Aarons' intention after a summer of training is to out-run everyone else in his year. But on the first day of school, a new girl boldly crosses over to the boys' side of the playground and outruns everyone. It doesn't seem like the best start to a friendship, but Jess and Leslie Burke become best friends. It doesn't matter to Jess that Leslie dresses strangely, or that her family has a lot more money than his – but no TV. Leslie has imagination. Together, she and Jess create Terabithia, a magical kingdom in the woods where the two of them reign as king and queen, and their imaginations set the only limits. But life isn't always as magical as their kingdom …

Artemis Fowl
Eoin Colfer

Artemis Fowl is a criminal genius. He has discovered the secrets of the fairies and is planning to make use of their technology for his own ends. But Holly Short, a member of the LEP force, is equally determined to stop him. The first in a highly entertaining series.

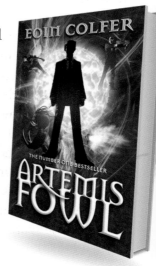

Sara's Face
Melvin Burgess

Sara is a beautiful but troubled teenager. She will do anything to be famous. Even though she is very pretty and has a boyfriend who genuinely loves her the way she is, Sara is not happy with her appearance. She meets a celebrity pop star, Jonathan Heat, whose life has been altered by plastic surgery. Heat invites Sara to live at his mansion, offering her plastic surgery and the chance to gain her own singing career and the fame she craves. But in this chilling tale all is not what it seems.

Invisible City
M.G. Harris

Joshua's life was pretty cool until his father was reported dead in an air crash in Mexico. Now Joshua has to find out if the death was really a tragic accident or if his father died because of an incredible, dangerous secret. Thrilling action-adventure.

Hana's Suitcase: A True Story
Karen Levine

When Fumiko Ishioka, curator of a Holocaust Education Centre in Japan, received an old suitcase with the name Hana Brady written on it, she became determined to find out more about its owner. She discovered that Hana was born in a small town in Czechoslovakia and that her parents and brother were taken to concentration camps. But what happened to Hana? The book switches over and back from the diary about Hana's life and Fumiko's search for the truth.

Pirates
Celia Rees

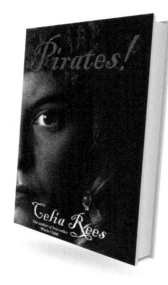

If you enjoyed the film *Pirates of the Caribbean* then this is the book for you. Fifteen-year-old Nancy Kington tells her story, which involves slavery, trickery, and eventually a life of piracy. This is a guaranteed page-turning read.

Stormbreaker
Anthony Horowitz

The first novel in Horowitz's hugely popular series about the boy-spy Alex Rider. Stylish and action-packed, a teenage James Bond.

Martyn Pig
Kevin Brooks

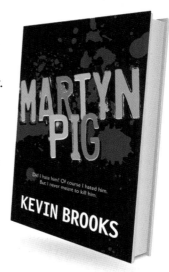

Martyn Pig has a violent, alcoholic father. During an argument Martyn accidentally kills his Dad in self-defence. His neighbour Alex helps him to hide the body. A darkly comic thriller that will keep you reading to the last page.

Coraline
Neil Gamain

Coraline stumbles on a parallel world, exactly like her own, except the people have button eyes. The further she travels in this world the more sinister it becomes. Will she be able to escape and return to her family? Weird, wonderful horror, with a dash of humour.

The Fire-Eaters
David Almond

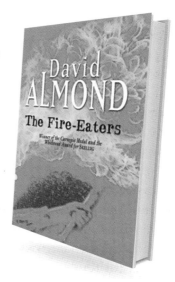

Set in the 1960s, this tells the story of a working-class boy who has won a scholarship to an expensive school where he struggles to fit in.

Holly Starcross
Berlie Doherty

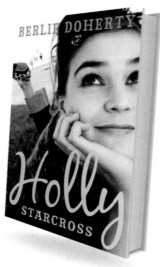

Holly Starcross can't quite work out who she is or who she wants to be. She lives with her mom, Henry (her mother's partner) and her half-brother and sisters. She has a great best friend and a crush on the cutest boy in school. Then her father, whom she hasn't seen for years, arrives and she has to face up to her past and start thinking more seriously about her future.

The Breadwinner
Deborah Ellis

Parvana lives in Afghanistan and is eleven. Her family is on the brink of starvation because her father is in prison. As a result she has to dress as a boy and go out to earn money and buy food. The Taliban rule and women are not allowed to leave their homes unless accompanied by a man. The adventures Parvana has and the dangers she endures keep you turning the pages.

Apache
Tanya Landman

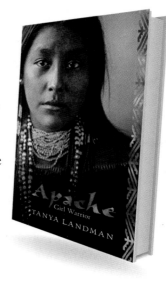

Siki's father failed to return from an ambush in Mexico leaving her an orphan of the Black Mountain Apache tribe at the age of fourteen. As the Mexican warriors had already killed her mother in a previous raid Siki already truly hates these people. But then her little brother Tazhi is brutally slain in front of her and she vows with all her heart to become an apache warrior and avenge his death. A thrilling read about courage in the face of suffering that is not always easy to read.

Private Peaceful
Michael Morpurgo

This is the story of two young brothers fighting in the trenches of World War I. Words can't describe what a good read this book is. If you liked *The Silver Sword* you'll love this.

The Penalty
Mal Peet

One of a series of books featuring Paul Faustino, South America's top sports journalist. While investigating the disappearance of San Juan's best teenage footballer he encounters corruption and evil that he doesn't expect. A tough and thought-provoking book.